Grammar in Literature

Susan Lavender • Stavroula Varella

Grammar in Literature

A Text-based Guide for Students

Susan Lavender
International English
University of Chichester
Chichester, UK

Stavroula Varella
School of Education, Communication and Society
King's College London
London, UK

ISBN 978-3-030-98892-0   ISBN 978-3-030-98893-7 (eBook)
https://doi.org/10.1007/978-3-030-98893-7

© The Editor(s) (if applicable) and The Author(s), under exclusive licence to Springer Nature Switzerland AG 2022
This work is subject to copyright. All rights are solely and exclusively licensed by the Publisher, whether the whole or part of the material is concerned, specifically the rights of translation, reprinting, reuse of illustrations, recitation, broadcasting, reproduction on microfilms or in any other physical way, and transmission or information storage and retrieval, electronic adaptation, computer software, or by similar or dissimilar methodology now known or hereafter developed.
The use of general descriptive names, registered names, trademarks, service marks, etc. in this publication does not imply, even in the absence of a specific statement, that such names are exempt from the relevant protective laws and regulations and therefore free for general use.
The publisher, the authors and the editors are safe to assume that the advice and information in this book are believed to be true and accurate at the date of publication. Neither the publisher nor the authors or the editors give a warranty, expressed or implied, with respect to the material contained herein or for any errors or omissions that may have been made. The publisher remains neutral with regard to jurisdictional claims in published maps and institutional affiliations.

This Palgrave Macmillan imprint is published by the registered company Springer Nature Switzerland AG.
The registered company address is: Gewerbestrasse 11, 6330 Cham, Switzerland

Preface

The book is entirely inspired by our own practical experiences of teaching English grammar to university students majoring in English Literature and in Creative Writing. It draws significantly on the successes and challenges we have encountered teaching grammar at undergraduate level. Our students often have different starting levels of knowledge of grammar and its metalanguage, conflicting attitudes to exploring grammar at all, and some reluctance to engage with a subject that, whilst indispensable for future progression, is quite heavy on technical information and, superficially, may seem to have little to do with other aspects of literature. It has always been our role to inspire them with our own interests in the roles of grammar in literature.

The book also reflects our experiences that those new to the field best explore how grammar works via close interaction with good single short texts followed by opportunities to experiment with and apply new knowledge in tasks which are interactive and motivating as well as fun.

The format of the book draws closely on our experiences of the processes by which we believe our students best engage with and find value in the study of grammar. We believe that an understanding of grammar is a vital tool for readers and writers. We also believe the study of grammar through literature to be both practical and inspiring.

Chichester, UK	Susan Lavender
London, UK	Stavroula Varella

Contents

1 English Grammar 1

Short Narrative 1 *Eveline* (1914) by James Joyce 7

2 Morphemes, Words and Lexical Categories 11

3 Nouns and Noun Phrases 19

4 Verbs 1: Tense and Aspect 27

5 Verbs 2: Modality, Catenation and Multi-Word Verbs 33

6 Verb Phrases 41

7 Basic Clauses 51

8 Sentences 57

9 Connecting Ideas: Clauses Revisited 65

10 Framing and Compiling: Sentences and the Text 75

11 Bringing It All Together 1: A Holistic Review of
Chaps. 2, 3, 4, 5, 6, 7, 8, 9 and 10 Based on Narrative 1 85

12 Bringing It All Together 2: A Holistic Appreciation of Narrative 1 . . 93

Short Narrative 2 *A Woman's College from the Outside* by Virginia
Woolf (1926) 99

13 Moving on 1: A Holistic Review of Chaps. 2, 3, 4, 5, 6, 7, 8, 9
and 10 Based on Narrative 2 103

14 Moving on 2: A Holistic Appreciation of Narrative 2 113

Suggested Answers 119
A Final Word 193
Recommendations for Further Reading 195
Glossary 199
Index. 207

Introduction to Grammar in Literature

Welcome to Grammar in Literature

This is a book for students of literature and creative writing who wish to understand more about the roles of grammar in literature. Working very closely with two selected texts, the book helps both to build your own knowledge of grammar and its metalanguage as well as to explore the roles of grammar as part of the creative processes which underpin good literature. Via a series of interactive tasks, based on two short narratives, the book guides you through the close symbiotic interfaces among grammar, writing and creativity. It encourages you to apply and experiment with what you learn in your own writing and to explore this with others. Our hope is to inspire you in both your reading and writing of literature. By the end of the book, you will have acquired a working knowledge of basic grammar metalanguage and have considered the affordances of grammar within creative writing processes.

Before starting Chap. 1 please take a moment to read the points below.

Our Approach to Grammar

This book is not a comprehensive grammar of English (there are already many of these which we recommend in later sections), but an exploration of the way grammar is used in particular narratives. We believe that approaching grammar in this special way

- Creates a level and engaging starting point for everyone;
- Focuses on the practical rather than the theoretical;
- Avoids the writing of special examples to illustrate a grammar point;
- Also avoids the cherry-picking of structurally uncomplex grammar examples: in the following chapters we work with the complexities and irregularities of the language used by our selected authors;

- Enables us to work at very close proximity with real texts so we can explore the details of the ways in which the narratives 'work';
- Enables us to come to know the selected narratives well so you are easily able to identify examples and explore their structures and impacts within a whole text;
- Is fundamentally engaging and useful to those studying literature and creative writing.

Our focus is on written text. For this reason, we have not included sections on features of pronunciation or prosody. There is an argument (which we fully accept) that these form part of the grammar of spoken English. They are, however, outside our remit here and are one of the reasons we have chosen to focus on the short narrative (which we suggest readers will normally access silently) rather than poetry.

As we focus on the creativity of the writing process, we also move beyond areas typically identified within grammar study. Later chapters in the book are thus entitled 'Connecting ideas' and 'Framing and compiling: sentences and the text'. In a sense, these titles might belong to the domains of stylistics (how grammar is used by an author in a particular work), discourse analysis (how language in particular contexts achieves coherence for its readers) and genre studies (the way structural elements combine to tell a narrative). We make no apology for this potential overlap. These later chapters are essential for exploring how grammar works in a particular narrative. In this sense, they are the justification for the study of aspects of grammar in previous chapters.

A Task-Based Approach to Grammar in Literature

We adopt a task-based 'learn-by-doing' approach to the mechanics of language. By studying grammar in relation to creativity, and by experimenting with your own linguistic and creative skills, you will come to appreciate the importance of language not only as a means of communication but also as an essential part of creative practice and literary composition. Most of the chapters conclude with creative writing activities. These are not just aimed at would-be creative writers. We believe it is only by putting grammar into practice for yourself that you come to see its potentials, and, to some extent, share the creative process of the writer.

Many of our activities are also interactive and encourage you to exchange ideas with others. This is a deliberate choice. Writing is normally a solitary process, with most works single authored. However, working interactively with others encourages conscious awareness and discussion of language and creative processes. It also provides a strong basis for engaging and interactive workshop/seminar sessions.

How This Book Is Different from Other Grammars of English

Essentially, this book invites you on a journey to explore the way, through its grammar, that a particular narrative 'works'. In so doing, it guides you through grammatical concepts related to English and it teaches you the relevant meta-language. We believe this book is unique in its task-based approach which relates grammar directly and consistently to selected texts so providing you with a basis for creative exploration of grammar in literature. The book moves beyond simply providing explanations and examples and encourages you to engage critically and creatively with aspects of grammar. It develops skills through which you can apply grammar awareness directly to textual analysis, your own creative writing, and related subjects involving literary appreciation, stylistics and criticism.

There are, of course, many other grammars of English. Our book is designed to be complementary to usage-based or descriptive grammars which generally aim to give wide coverage of the grammatical features of the language and range from the very basic (aimed usually at young and lay readers) to the highly technical aimed at an informed, academic audience. We recommend some of the best of these for follow-up work in later sections of our book. However, they are concerned with 'English at large' while our focus in this book is to introduce grammar via an exploration of how it 'works' in particular texts. In most descriptive grammars, the addition of carefully chosen examples, realistic as they might be, can say something about current usage but almost nothing about the cohesiveness and beauty of the language which forms our focus here. We also find the theoretical grammars can be over-challenging, if not irrelevant, for those who are basically interested in literature and writing.

It is worth mentioning here two other common kinds of grammars which our book is not. Our entirely text-based approach means we avoid the prescriptivism of several writing and style guides (often produced for a lay audience). Traditional or prescriptive grammars have (quite rightly) fallen out of use, at least in educational contexts. We believe our text-based approach ensures we avoid prescriptiveness, and we believe that you need to appreciate English grammar for what it can do rather than how people might claim it should be.

There are other applied grammars like ours, but they are often combined with other aspects of language such as vocabulary and pronunciation, and many are directed at English grammar for users of other languages. Our book is, essentially, an applied approach to learning about grammar for students of English literature and/or creative writing who, in our experience, are mostly near-native or native users of the language and, therefore, good users of grammar but less aware of its significance for communication and creativity.

A Note on Grammatical Terminology

Grammatical terminology is a metalanguage. We believe familiarity with this metalanguage is important for three reasons.

i. It enables those relatively new to the field to understand how others conceive of language structures and how they suggest structures can be described and grouped.
ii. It enables you to consult and work with the large body of grammar reference materials.
iii. Understanding how the metalanguage is applied itself promotes your own insights into language use and can thus scaffold your discussion of these uses.

As the metalanguage of grammar can often be a stumbling block, we assume no prior knowledge, we introduce terms only as we need and use them, and we recycle them via creative tasks.

Of course, not all grammarians completely agree on all terminology and fashions change. Where there is doubt on which term should be applied or where analysis may be ambiguous, we have tried to acknowledge this. In general, we work with particular terms which seem most logical to us and to exploration of our narratives. Whenever there is ambiguity and views may differ, we try to indicate this in our 'check the basics' sections.

Our Choice of Texts

Literature is normally the most planned kind of writing. Simply put, it showcases use of grammar. This is why we have chosen to work with short narratives. (By short narrative we effectively mean a short story of fewer than 2000 words.) Because of their length, short narratives are not only highly accessible and designed to be read in a single sitting, but they are also highly sculpted by their authors. In brief, they often showcase prose writing at its best. The short narrative is where prose comes closest to poetry, whilst, at the same time, retaining the syntactical and grammatical features typical of written text. All these features combine to make short narratives ideal for our purposes.

Our main text is *Eveline* by James Joyce, which first appeared in the collection *Dubliners*, published by Grant Richards in London in 1914. We work with the same narrative from Chaps. 1, 2, 3, 4, 5, 6, 7, 8, 9, 10, 11 and 12 so that we can fully explore its possibilities and so that you will come to know it well enough to perceive the full range of its crafting. We hope you will appreciate Joyce's narrative for its timeless themes and cherish it for its elegance and ingenuity.

Our second narrative is *A Woman's College from the Outside* by Virginia Woolf (1926) which we use in our review Chaps. 13 and 14. We select this text as it shares several features with the first in terms of creativity, theme and style. These make it a good choice to review the ideas explored in Chaps. 1, 2, 3, 4, 5, 6, 7, 8, 9, 10, 11 and 12, and then, at a more holistic level, to provide an example for further exploration of grammatical features in literature.

We could, of course, have based our book on very many other excellent short texts. We choose to work with these particular texts as they meet three essential criteria.

- They are, we believe, excellent examples of their genre (short narrative) which have stood the test of time well and are still much read and enjoyed today.
- They are, of course, short which makes them easy to work with and recall.
- Most importantly, we think they are narratives that you will enjoy, engage with and find interesting to discuss.

Both texts are out of UK copyright which means they are widely available, and we are able to print them in this book. If you would like a free download of the texts please see Project Gutenberg.

We frequently quote from the first narrative and adapt it for the purposes of practice and consolidation. You can find the full text after Chap. 1 and you will need to refer to it as you work through each subsequent chapter. The second narrative occurs after Chap. 12 and provides the work for our final two review chapters.

The purpose of our book is not, of course, to limit you to these single texts, but to use them to encourage you to explore the genre further and work with your own narratives. Please see our recommendations for further exploration of short narratives at the end of the book.

The Structure of the Book

For reasons of familiarity and in line with orderings traditionally adopted by descriptive grammars, we choose to work from smallest to largest. We therefore begin our exploration with the smallest units we consider by starting at a lexical (i.e. word) level. We then move through phrases to clauses and sentences, finally focussing on text level coherence and notions of writer style and stance in the whole text. Our approach is, though, cumulative rather than linear as each chapter assumes and builds on understanding of previous chapters. For this reason, it is best to work through the book in order. As mentioned above, our use of metalanguage is therefore also cumulative.

We use the convention of italic font for all examples from the narratives and bold to highlight new metalanguage as we introduce it. We then include, at the back of the book, an alphabetical reference glossary of all the highlighted terminology. We intend this as a quick ready reference and aide memoire rather than an in-depth account. For this reason, we conclude the book with a section on suggested further reading which includes reference to other grammar books, and also stylistics and creative writing textbooks for you to explore. After finishing the tasks in this book, we strongly recommend you consider the application of the areas to other literary work as well as your own writing. You will also find ideas for this at the back of the book.

Chapter 1 is an introductory chapter that presents the aims and distinctive features of the book. It introduces you to the notion of grammar, before examining the importance of grammar for writing. It shows how all good authors 'know their grammar'; how good writing is the result of careful consideration of alternative forms and structures; and how informed linguistic choices have major impacts on the aesthetics of a text. By the end of the chapter, you should feel inspired to learn more about the grammar of English, and to subsequently explore the idea of linguistic choice in your appreciation of literary texts as well as in your own writing.

Chapters 2, 3, 4, 5, 6, 7, 8, 9 and 10 are similar in structure, each focusing on a key grammatical aspect linked to particular elements in the first text and ending with suggestions for further exploration and application of the knowledge you gain into your own writing. We begin our exploration with word level analysis, moving on to phrases and clauses and, finally, to sentences and the whole text. Essentially, then, each chapter provides a lens to permit a focus on an aspect of grammar, whilst our use of a single text maintains a holistic and unifying view.

Chapters 11 and 12 are review chapters. We explore Joyce's narrative in its entirety with a focus on how on the grammar features explored in preceding chapters cumulatively and interactively create our interpretation and appreciation of the text.

Chapters 13 and 14 are also review chapters but use our second text *A Woman's College from the Outside* by Virginia Woolf. They encourage you to recall and apply areas covered in Chaps. 1, 2, 3, 4, 5, 6, 7, 8, 9, 10, 11 and 12 to a new narrative. Finally, Chap. 14 encourages you to apply your knowledge and insights from the first thirteen chapters as a jumping off point for you to explore (and create!) other narratives, and other genres.

The book thus covers a core syllabus of grammar and its metalanguage that will also enable you to progress in your study of more advanced subjects in language and linguistics (e.g. discourse analysis, stylistics, genre studies), while, at the same time, inviting you to engage with material that you find stimulating, meaningful, and applicable.

We conclude with a section of our suggested answers to the tasks. Clearly, there are usually no rights or wrongs, but we hope our thoughts will add to your own. This section is deliberately extensive and even sometimes controversial to encourage your own exploration and reflection. You will, of course, benefit most from the answer section after you have given thought to the tasks yourself!

The Structure of the Chapters

For simplicity, each chapter follows a similar format of five sections as noted in the box below.

Chapter section	Rationale
In essence	This short section consists of a simple overview of the content and aims of the chapter.
Check the basics	This section provides a brief explanation of the grammar using illustrations from the selected narrative and introduces and reviews the necessary metalanguage.
Textual analysis of the narrative	This section provides a series of guided tasks to encourage you to explore the focus of the chapter in the selected narrative. You apply your learning to the narrative.
Exploring & writing	In this section you undertake a series of interactive tasks (with your peers) which encourage your own creative exploration of the grammar focus of the chapter. This section is designed to be fun and motivating and invites you to explore the impacts of the grammar covered in the chapter.
Review & reflection	This final section provides a consolidation of the chapter to encourage you to review the content and select your own salient points. We believe it is often only after reflection that points of personal salience and understanding emerge.

Suggested Ways of Using the Book

The book is mainly designed to be used in workshop or seminar format with each chapter covered in one session. Although many of the tasks are also suitable for individuals working alone, you are most likely to derive enjoyment and challenge from working through the interactive tasks with like-minded others.

In producing the materials we have envisaged the book being used for a standard semester pattern of around 14 weeks with individual class session lasting about two hours and participants devoting around four additional hours to preparation and follow-up tasks. The in-class tasks require you to work interactively with the selected narratives and with each other. In our experience, after the preliminary introductory session, starting each session by reviewing the creative tasks and reflective reviews from the previous session works well. For this reason, we estimate that the 10 chapters and the final reflection/reviews can be covered in approximately 12 sessions. The final review chapters can be completed alone or as an interactive group session. They can also act as good preparation for a summative assessment.

The table below overviews our own use of the materials with a 2 hour-per-week seminar/workshop group over a 14-week semester. Apart from the first and final sessions, it indicates a typical way of working through the materials, with participants expected to devote 4 hours of their time outside formal sessions for preparation and follow-up activities. In our experience, the sessions work best if participants bring their completed work from the 'Review and reflection' section for checking and discussion in the subsequent session, and also prepare the 'In essence' and 'Check the basics' sections for each new chapter in advance.

Pre-session student preparation	Participants prepare by reviewing the 'In essence' and 'Check the basics' sections for the upcoming chapter.
In-session first hour	Discuss 'Review & reflection' from the previous session. Participants are encouraged to discuss their ideas and raise any questions. Review the 'In essence' and 'Check the basics' sections for the new chapter and then work through the 'Textual analysis of the narrative' with the group.
In-session second hour	Complete tasks from the 'Exploring & writing' sections. These work best with students working in pairs and small groups with plenary workshop-based feedback on each task.
Post-session student follow-up	Participants complete any 'Exploring & writing' tasks as necessary. Participants complete the 'Review & reflection' section for group discussion and/or feedback at the beginning of their next session.

This sequence forms a cyclical approach in which tasks and discussions from the previous session are a starting point for each new session. Participants are encouraged to take responsibility for bringing previous work to each session and for pre-preparing 'Check the basics' sections.

Please note it is not necessary or normally possible, within a two-hour weekly session, to complete all the 'Exploring & writing' tasks. We suggest participants can be offered choices.

A Final Thought

We hope you find this book an enjoyable and engaging introduction to English Grammar in literature that provides you with both sound knowledge of the mechanics of the language and a reference guide to its terminology. Mainly, though, we hope the book will encourage you to explore the creative interfaces between grammar and literature. We hope you will become aware of ways in which our grammar affords us all kinds of possibilities in writing and expression. In essence, we write the ways we do because of the possibilities afforded by the grammar of our language, and good literature is sculpted as an outcome of the structures and complexities offered by that language.

We have designed this book and its creative tasks to be enjoyable: we hope you find them so!

Chapter 1
English Grammar

In Essence

This initial chapter explores your understanding of the meanings and uses of grammar. It outlines our overall approach to grammar and also gives you experience of the ways we will work in following chapters. The chapter thus prepares you to undertake the tasks on Joyce's narrative in Chaps. 2, 3, 4, 5, 6, 7, 8, 9, 10, 11 and 12 and on Woolf's narrative in Chaps. 13 and 14.

Check the Basics

What Is Grammar?

There are at least three answers to this question.

First of all, we need to think about 'the grammar' of a language, the system by which the **words**, or indeed parts of words (**morphemes**) of a language are organised into larger units such as **phrases, clauses and sentences**. Such a system is characteristic of any natural language, part and parcel of what linguistic communication is, and therefore, to quote Trask 'perceived as existing independently of any attempt at describing it.'[1]

Secondly, we could refer to the actual description of such as system, dependent on a consistent set of identifiable patterns in the organisation of words and phrases and exemplified as a set of rules that determine habitual and/or acceptable use in a particular language. This sense of 'grammar' is best understood in the context of

---

[1] R.L. Trask (1993), *A Dictionary of Grammatical Terms in Linguistics*. London: Routledge (p. 122).

© The Author(s), under exclusive license to Springer Nature Switzerland AG 2022
S. Lavender, S. Varella, *Grammar in Literature*,
https://doi.org/10.1007/978-3-030-98893-7_1

analysis of individual languages and, sometimes, varieties of these languages. While all languages have grammars in the first sense of the word, some non-standard language varieties don't (yet) have documented 'grammars' in the second sense of the word.

Finally, there's Grammar as a branch of **Linguistics**, the study of language, which is conventionally distinguished into **Morphology** (the study of word structure) and **Syntax** (the study of sentence structure). Students of linguistics will normally find themselves studying grammar from a particular framework of linguistic theory, such as Chomsky's Generative Grammar or Halliday's Systemic Functional Grammar, landmarks in Linguistics scholarship with their diverse foci respectively on language as a faculty of the human mind and on language as a communicative system.

Textual Analysis

Task A
1. What do authors think about grammar? Do they consciously consider it when writing? Discuss your ideas.
2. Now read the comments below and discuss again in the light of these comments.

   i. Joan Didion[2] reflects on Grammar thus:

   Grammar is a piano I play by ear, since I seem to have been out of school the year the rules were mentioned. All I know about grammar is its infinite power. To shift the structure of a sentence alters the meaning of that sentence, as definitely and inflexibly as the position of a camera alters the meaning of the object photographed. Many people know about camera angles now, but not so many know about sentences. The arrangement of the words matters, and the arrangement you want can be found in the picture in your mind. The picture dictates the arrangement. The picture dictates whether this will be a sentence with or without clauses, a sentence that ends hard or a dying-fall sentence, long or short, active or passive. The picture tells you how to arrange the words and the arrangement of the words tells you, or tells me, what's going on in the picture. Nota bene.
   It tells you.
   You don't tell it.

The 'picture in your mind' is something many writers can relate to. It's a combination of authorial instinct, an often unconscious but no less real consideration of diction, sentence structure, and style, and a more deliberate process of active choice-making. If what you write is right, you will know.

   ii. Here is a piece of advice from a commercial website for writers:[3]

   Most forms of English instruction emphasise rules and memorisation; however, I recommend a more instinctual method of mastery. Rather than mapping out sentences or

---

[2] Joan Didion (1977), 'Why I Write'. The London Magazine. Vol.17. No.2.
[3] Saga Briggs (2016), 'Five Ways to Develop an Ear for English Grammar'. ProWritingAid.com. Available at https://prowritingaid.com/art/327/5-Ways-to-Develop-an-"Ear"-for-English-Grammar.aspx [last accessed 9/2/21].

memorising confusing and often inconsistent rules, you can improve your communication skills by simply tapping into the logic of rhythm and structure.

iii. In her best-selling guidebook on reading literature, Francine Prose[4] tells the story of a writer who, when interviewed by an agent, said that *'what he really cared about, what he wanted most of all was to write … really great sentences.'* It's an unusual story, she says, because *'to talk about sentences is to have a conversation about something far more meaningful and personal to most authors'*. Yet as she later reaffirms writers read other writers *'for no other reason than to marvel at the skill with which they can put together the sort of sentences that move us to read closely, to disassemble and reassemble them, much the way a mechanic might learn from an engine by taking it apart'*.

Later the same author puts forward this idea:
> *One essential and telling difference between learning from a style manual and learning from literature is that any how-to book will, almost by definition, tell you how not to write. In that way, manuals of style are a little like writing workshops, and have the same disadvantage – a pedagogy that involves warnings about what might be broken and directions on how to fix it – as opposed to learning from literature, which teaches by positive model.*

3. Which of the descriptions of the relationships between grammar and writers do you think most insightful and/or most helpful?

In the following chapters, we hope that you can also learn 'by positive model', while simultaneously acquiring the metalanguage that will be necessary as you proceed from foundational to more advanced studies in grammar and textual analysis.

Exploring & Writing

Task A
1. What does grammar mean to you? Discuss with a partner.
2. Share your answers as a group. Are the views your express covered by the three main points in the 'Check the basics' section above?

Task B
1. Below are seven common units of grammatical analysis. Number the items from smallest unit to largest unit.

   - Paragraph
   - Clause
   - Morpheme
   - Word
   - Text
   - Sentence
   - Phrase

---

[4] Francine Prose (2012), *Reading Like a Writer. A Guide for People who Love Books and for Those Who Want to Write Them.* London: Aurum Press.

2. These are the units we will work with in the following chapters of this book. Check your understanding of each with a partner. Refer to the Glossary at the back of this book if you need to.

Task C

1. Work with a partner to discuss the comment below.

    Simply choosing the right words to convey a message (or a sentiment, or a reflection) cannot, of itself, guarantee effective writing. Linguistic choice is about words, but it is also about grammar. It is the combination of word choice and sentence structure that together allow writers to sculpt sentences and texts that are lively, energetic, powerful, lucid or poetic etc.

2. Below are two well-known paragraphs written by Charles Dickens. Work with a partner. Choose one of the texts and then consider the questions below in relation to the text you have chosen.

    i. What is the topic of your text?
    ii. How does the language support the topic?
    iii. Why do you think your text has become a well-known example of a well-crafted text?
    iv. Think back to the discussion of grammar earlier in this chapter. Relate your text to the discussion.
    v. Think back to the discussion on how writers work. Can you also relate this discussion to your text?

Text A: Charles Dickens: *A Tale of Two Cities* (opening, paragraph 1):

It was the best of times, it was the worst of times, it was the age of wisdom, it was the age of foolishness, it was the epoch of belief, it was the epoch of incredulity, it was the season of Light, it was the season of Darkness, it was the spring of hope, it was the winter of despair, we had everything before us, we had nothing before us, we were all going direct to Heaven, we were all going direct the other way – in short, the period was so far like the present period, that some of its noisiest authorities insisted on its being received, for good or for evil, in the superlative degree of comparison only.

Text B: Charles Dickens: *Bleak House* (opening, paragraph 2):

Fog everywhere. Fog up the river, where it flows among green aits and meadows; fog down the river, where it rolls defiled among the tiers of shipping and the waterside pollutions of a great (and dirty) city. Fog on the Essex marshes, fog on the Kentish heights. Fog creeping into the cabooses of collier-brigs; fog lying out on the yards, and hovering in the rigging of great ships; fog drooping on the gunwales of barges and small boats. Fog in the eyes and throats of ancient Greenwich pensioners, wheezing by the firesides of their wards; fog in the stem and bowl of the afternoon pipe of the wrathful skipper, down in his close cabin; fog cruelly pinching the toes and fingers of his shivering little apprentice boy on deck. Chance people on the bridges peeping over the parapets into a nether sky of fog, with fog all round them, as if they were up in a balloon, and hanging in the misty clouds.

3. Change partners. (It does not matter if you have previously worked with the same or different texts.) Discuss your responses to the questions above together.

Task D
1. Work with a partner. Choose one of the themes below and write a paragraph of at least 4 sentences in the style of Dickens (as above).

   Love
   Home
   Age (young or old)

2. Share your writing with the whole group.
3. With your partner again and discuss the questions below.

   How does it feel to write with someone?
   What did it make easier than writing alone?
   What was more difficult?
   Were you conscious of drawing on any of the themes of this chapter as you discussed your writing?
   What does it mean to write in the style of someone?

Review & Reflection

Task A
What are the main points you recall from Chap. 1?

Task B
Explain to your group your own understanding and/or experience of Didion's observation:

To shift the structure of a sentence alters the meaning of that sentence, as definitely and inflexibly as the position of a camera alters the meaning of the object photographed.

Short Narrative 1
Eveline (1914) by James Joyce

We present our first short narrative, *Eveline*, taken from *Dubliners,* a collection of short stories by James Joyce. Published by Grant Richards in London in 1914, the stories are all set in Joyce's contemporary Dublin. *Eveline* tells the story of a nineteen-year-old woman who is weighing her decision to leave her native Dublin and move with her lover in Buenos Aires, Argentina.

We base most of our chapters on this narrative. As explained in the introduction, we use the narrative (in Chaps. 2, 3, 4, 5, 6, 7, 8, 9 and 10,) to explore aspects of grammar from morphology to sentence and text-level construction. Chapters 11 and 12 then provide a holistic overview of how the text 'works'.

Eveline

She sat at the window watching the evening invade the avenue. Her head was leaned against the window curtains and in her nostrils was the odour of dusty cretonne. She was tired.

Few people passed. The man out of the last house passed on his way home; she heard his footsteps clacking along the concrete pavement and afterwards crunching on the cinder path before the new red houses. One time there used to be a field there in which they used to play every evening with other people's children. Then a man from Belfast bought the field and built houses in it – not like their little brown houses but bright brick houses with shining roofs. The children of the avenue used to play together in that field – the Devines, the Waters, the Dunns, little Keogh the cripple, she and her brothers and sisters. Ernest, however, never played: he was too grown up. Her father used often to hunt them in out of the field with his blackthorn stick; but usually little Keogh used to keep nix and call out when he saw her father coming. Still they seemed to have been rather happy then. Her father was not so bad then; and besides, her mother was alive. That was a long time ago; she and her brothers and sisters were all grown up her mother was dead. Tizzie Dunn was dead, too, and the Waters had gone back to England. Everything changes. Now she was going to go away like the others, to leave her home.

Home! She looked round the room, reviewing all its familiar objects which she had dusted once a week for so many years, wondering where on earth all the dust came from. Perhaps she would never see again those familiar objects from which she had never dreamed of being divided. And yet during all those years she had never found out the name of the priest whose yellowing photograph hung on the wall above the broken harmonium beside the coloured print of the promises made to Blessed Margaret Mary Alacoque. He had been a school friend of her father. Whenever he showed the photograph to a visitor her father used to pass it with a casual word:

"He is in Melbourne now."

She had consented to go away, to leave her home. Was that wise? She tried to weigh each side of the question. In her home anyway she had shelter and food; she had those whom she had known all her life about her. Of course she had to work hard, both in the house and at business. What would they say of her in the Stores when they found out that she had run away with a fellow? Say she was a fool, perhaps; and her place would be filled up by advertisement. Miss Gavan would be glad. She had always had an edge on her, especially whenever there were people listening.

"Miss Hill, don't you see these ladies are waiting?"

"Look lively, Miss Hill, please."

She would not cry many tears at leaving the Stores.

But in her new home, in a distant unknown country, it would not be like that. Then she would be married – she, Eveline. People would treat her with respect then. She would not be treated as her mother had been. Even now, though she was over nineteen, she sometimes felt herself in danger of her father's violence. She knew it was that that had given her the palpitations. When they were growing up he had never gone for her like he used to go for Harry and Ernest, because she was a girl; but latterly he had begun to threaten her and say what he would do to her only for her dead mother's sake. And now she had nobody to protect her. Ernest was dead and Harry, who was in the church decorating business, was nearly always down somewhere in the country. Besides, the invariable squabble for money on Saturday nights had begun to weary her unspeakably. She always gave her entire wages – seven shillings – and Harry always sent up what he could but the trouble was to get any money from her father. He said she used to squander the money, that she had no head, that he wasn't going to give her his hard-earned money to throw about the streets, and much more, for he was usually fairly bad on Saturday night. In the end he would give her the money and ask her had she any intention of buying Sunday's dinner. Then she had to rush out as quickly as she could and do her marketing, holding her black leather purse tightly in her hand as she elbowed her way through the crowds and returning home late under her load of provisions. She had hard work to keep the house together and to see that the two young children who had been left to her charge went to school regularly and got their meals regularly. It was hard work – a hard life – but now that she was about to leave it she did not find it a wholly undesirable life.

She was about to explore another life with Frank. Frank was very kind, manly, open-hearted. She was to go away with him by the night-boat to be his wife and to live with him in Buenos Ayres where he had a home waiting for her. How well she remembered the first time she had seen him; he was lodging in a house on the main road where she used to visit. It seemed a few weeks ago. He was standing at the gate, his peaked cap pushed back on his head and his hair tumbled forward over a face of bronze. Then they had come to know each other. He used to meet her outside the Stores every evening and see her home. He took her to see The Bohemian Girl and she felt elated as she sat in an unaccustomed part of the theatre with him. He was awfully fond of music and sang a little. People knew that they were courting and, when he sang about the lass that loves a sailor, she always felt pleasantly confused. He used to call her Poppens out of fun. First of all it had been an excitement for her to have a fellow and then she had begun to like him. He had tales of distant countries. He had started as a deck boy at a pound a month on a ship of the Allan Line going out to Canada. He told her the names of the ships he had been on and the names of the different services. He had sailed through the Straits of Magellan and he told her stories of the terrible Patagonians. He had fallen on his feet in Buenos Ayres, he said, and had come over to the old country just for a holiday. Of course, her father had found out the affair and had forbidden her to have anything to say to him.

"I know these sailor chaps," he said.

One day he had quarrelled with Frank and after that she had to meet her lover secretly.

The evening deepened in the avenue. The white of two letters in her lap grew indistinct. One was to Harry; the other was to her father. Ernest had been her favourite but she liked Harry too. Her father was becoming old lately, she noticed; he would miss her. Sometimes he could be very nice. Not long before, when she had been laid up for a day, he had read her out a ghost story and made toast for her at the fire. Another day, when their mother was alive, they had all gone for a picnic to the Hill of Howth. She remembered her father putting on her mother's bonnet to make the children laugh.

Her time was running out but she continued to sit by the window, leaning her head against the window curtain, inhaling the odour of dusty cretonne. Down far in the avenue she could hear a street organ playing. She knew the air. Strange that it should come that very night to remind her of the promise to her mother, her promise to keep the home together as long as she could. She remembered the last night of her mother's illness; she was again in the close dark room at the other side of the hall and outside she heard a melancholy air of Italy. The organ-player had been ordered to go away and given sixpence. She remembered her father strutting back into the sickroom saying:

"Damned Italians! coming over here!"

As she mused the pitiful vision of her mother's life laid its spell on the very quick of her being – that life of commonplace sacrifices closing in final craziness. She trembled as she heard again her mother's voice saying constantly with foolish insistence:

"DerevaunSeraun! DerevaunSeraun!"

She stood up in a sudden impulse of terror. Escape! She must escape! Frank would save her. He would give her life, perhaps love, too. But she wanted to live. Why should she be unhappy? She had a right to happiness. Frank would take her in his arms, fold her in his arms. He would save her.

She stood among the swaying crowd in the station at the North Wall. He held her hand and she knew that he was speaking to her, saying something about the passage over and over again. The station was full of soldiers with brown baggages. Through the wide doors of the sheds she caught a glimpse of the black mass of the boat, lying in beside the quay wall, with illumined portholes. She answered nothing. She felt her cheek pale and cold and, out of a maze of distress, she prayed to God to direct her, to show her what was her duty. The boat blew a long mournful whistle into the mist. If she went, tomorrow she would be on the sea with Frank, steaming towards Buenos Ayres. Their passage had been booked. Could she still draw back after all he had done for her? Her distress awoke a nausea in her body and she kept moving her lips in silent fervent prayer.

A bell clanged upon her heart. She felt him seize her hand:

"Come!"

All the seas of the world tumbled about her heart. He was drawing her into them: he would drown her. She gripped with both hands at the iron railing. "Come!"

No! No! No! It was impossible. Her hands clutched the iron in frenzy. Amid the seas she sent a cry of anguish.

"Eveline! Evvy!"

He rushed beyond the barrier and called to her to follow. He was shouted at to go on but he still called to her. She set her white face to him, passive, like a helpless animal. Her eyes gave him no sign of love or farewell or recognition.

Chapter 2
Morphemes, Words and Lexical Categories

In Essence

In this chapter you study the opening paragraphs of *Eveline* and identify morphemes and lexical categories. You explore how Joyce builds echoes into the narrative via morphemic structure and how he uses lexical sets and balances of lexical categories to tell his story and to create the style and tone of the text. You then explore your own uses of these features when creating the opening of a narrative.

Check the Basics

For our purposes here, a **word** is the single smallest unit of language that is normally used alone. For example, in the narrative we find the word *Escape!* used as a complete sentence.

The beginning of the narrative also has the words *footsteps* and *played*. These are different from *escape* in that they can be divided into constituent **morphemes** i.e. foot + steps and play + ed.

Escape is a single word and also a single morpheme. This combination is called a **free morpheme** as the morpheme can stand alone, i.e. work as a word on its own.

Footsteps is thus a combination of two free morphemes. *Played* is made up of the free morpheme *play* and the **bound morpheme** *ed*. Bound morphemes cannot act as words on their own. See other examples of bound morphemes below.

Word	Free morpheme	Bound morpheme
watching	*watch*	*ing*
curtains	*curtain*	*s*
passed	*pass*	*ed*

© The Author(s), under exclusive license to Springer Nature
Switzerland AG 2022
S. Lavender, S. Varella, *Grammar in Literature*,
https://doi.org/10.1007/978-3-030-98893-7_2

Word	Free morpheme	Bound morpheme
illness	*ill*	*ness*
indistinct	*distinct*	*in*

As is clear from the table, bound morphemes can be placed before or after free morphemes (called **prefixes** and **suffixes** respectively) and are the result of two process: (a) **Derivation**, which creates a new word (ill > illness, distinct > indistinct) or (b) **inflection,** which adds a grammatical nuance to the original word (curtain > curtains, pass > passed).

Lexical categories (sometimes referred to as **parts of speech** or **word classes**) represent a way of organising words according to their grammatical **form**, i.e. their appearance, morphological structure and position in a sentence) and their grammatical **function**, i.e. their role or purpose in a sentence, motivated by their meaning. We introduce the notion of function in Chap. 3 and develop it further in Chap. 7. The general principle to remember here is that **form** and **function** are different. This chapter deals primarily with form.

Compare the three examples below which show how words of different categories are formed in the narrative from the **free morpheme** *dust*.

*The odour of **dusty** cretonne.* (**adjective**)
*She had **dusted** once a week.* (**verb**)
*Where on earth all the **dust** came from.* (**noun**)

It is important to note that the classification of an item into a particular lexical category depends on the use of a word in a particular context. In other words, the classification of a word is not an inherent part of the word itself e.g.

*She had to **work** hard* (verb)
*She had hard **work*** (noun)

Some lexical categories (**nouns, verbs, adjectives, adverbs**) are **open categories** because new items can easily be added to them, e.g. 'alcopop' (noun), 'defriend' (verb). The other lexical categories (**prepositions, pronouns, determiners, conjunctions and interjections**) are **closed categories** as they do not readily admit new items: e.g. *on, for, of* (prepositions); *you, she, them* (pronouns); *a, the, this, some* (determiners); *and, but, when* (conjunctions); *Oh! Yes! Ouch!* (interjections).

It is often helpful to think of open categories as containing **lexical or content words** and closed categories containing **grammatical or function words**. Almost all texts use a mixture of open and closed categories.

The following sentences are from the third paragraph of *Eveline*. The table below shows the functions of the words as they are used here.

> *Home! She looked round the room, reviewing all its familiar objects which she had dusted once a week for so many years, wondering where on earth all the dust came from. Perhaps she would never see again those familiar objects from which she had never dreamed of being divided. And yet during all those years she had never found out the name of the priest whose yellowing photograph hung on the wall above the broken harmonium beside the coloured print of the promises made to Blessed Margaret Mary Alacoque.*

Nouns people, things, emotions	*home, room, objects, dust, years, earth, name, priest, photograph, wall, harmonium, print, promises*
Verbs actions, states of affairs	*looked, reviewing, had dusted, wondering, would see, had dreamt, being, had found out, hung*
Adjectives lexical words describing nouns	*familiar, yellowing, broken, coloured*
Adverbs lexical words describing verbs e.g. how, how often, how much etc.	*once a week, never, again*
Pronouns words which can take the place of a noun	*she, which, whose*
Prepositions words which describe the relationship of something to a noun	*for, on, from, during, above, besides, to*
Determiners words which come before nouns to specify or identify the noun	*the, all, its, many, those*
Conjunctions words which join phrases, clauses and sentences	*perhaps, and yet*

Textual Analysis of the Narrative

Task A
Read the second paragraph of *Eveline*; then do the tasks below.

> *Few people passed. The man out of the last house passed on his way home; she heard his footsteps clacking along the concrete pavement and afterwards crunching on the cinder path before the new red houses. One time there used to be a field there in which they used to play every evening with other people's children. Then a man from Belfast bought the field and built houses in it—not like their little brown houses but bright brick houses with shining roofs. The children of the avenue used to play together in that field—the Devines, the Waters, the Dunns, little Keogh the cripple, she and her brothers and sisters. Ernest, however, never played: he was too grown up. Her father used often to hunt them in out of the field with his blackthorn stick; but usually little Keogh used to keep nix and call out when he saw her father coming. Still they seemed to have been rather happy then. Her father was not so bad then; and besides, her mother was alive. That was a long time ago; she and her brothers and sisters were all grown up her mother was dead. Tizzie Dunn was dead, too, and the Waters had gone back to England. Everything changes. Now she was going to go away like the others, to leave her home.*

1. Look at the words below; they are taken from the paragraph in the order they appear. Do you agree that, as printed in the table (therefore out of context) all of these words are nouns? Look again at the whole sentences in the narrative. Which of these words have a different function?

> *people – man – house – way – home – footsteps – concrete – pavement – cinder – path – houses – time – field – evening – children – man – Belfast – houses – brick – houses – roofs – children – avenue – field – Devines – Waters – Dunns – Keogh – cripple – brothers – sisters – Ernest – father – field – blackthorn – stick*

2. What patterns do you notice in the meanings of the nouns?
3. Which of the nouns are plurals?
4. Nouns which use the name of a person or place are known as **proper nouns**. In the second paragraph, when does Joyce use proper nouns? Who is referred to by name? Who is referred to by other means, such as relationships? What effects does this have?
5. Identify the other proper nouns in the narrative. How are they used throughout the narrative?

Task B
1. Here are some of the adjectives from the same paragraph. Which nouns are they used with?

last – new – red – little – brown – bright – shining – little

2. In the phrases below the adjectives are used in two different ways. What's the difference?

   i. *not like their <u>little brown</u> houses but <u>bright brick</u> houses with <u>shining</u> roofs*
   ii. *Her father was not so <u>bad</u>*
   iii. *her mother was <u>alive</u>*

   What are the effects?
   Whose perspective do you think these adjectives are applied from?
   In the first example the adjectives are used **attributively** (i.e. they precede the noun they describe) and in the following two **predicatively** (i.e. they follow the noun they describe). Which way are most of the adjectives in the paragraph used?

Task C
1. Here is the first part of the paragraph without the verbs. Try to replace them from memory.

   Still they _____ rather happy then. Her father _____ not so bad then; and besides, her mother _____ alive. That _____ a long time ago; she and her brothers and sisters _____ all grown up her mother _____ dead. Tizzie Dunn _____ dead, too, and the Waters _____ back to England. Everything _____. Now she was _____ like the others, _____ her home.

2. What are the effects of taking the verbs out of the text?
3. What's the difference in form and meaning between these verbs: *'to go away'*, *'to leave'*?
4. What other multi-word verbs in the narrative are formed by more than one word? What do they have in common?
5. The following two sentences occur near the end of the narrative. Look at the 6 words in bold. Decide if they each function as a verb or an adjective.

   *She **stood** among the **swaying** crowd in the station at the North Wall. He **held** her hand and she **knew** that he was **speaking** to her, **saying** something about the passage over and over again.*

Task D
1. Adverbs of time (e.g. *then*) are used frequently in this paragraph. Why do you think time is significant?
2. Which other types of adverbs can you recognize in the narrative? (Types refer to manner, place, frequency, negation, time, degree, probability)
3. It is estimated that nouns make up 37% of total words in an average English text.[1]

    What do you think is the percentage of nouns in the paragraph above?
    Calculate (roughly) the noun to verb ratio in the paragraph.
    Calculate (roughly) the adjective to noun ratio in the paragraph.
    Calculate (roughly) the adverb to verb ratio in the paragraph.
4. Discuss how the choice of words and lexical categories help build the narrative.

Task E
1. *The Waters had **gone** back to England*: *gone* is formed (irregularly) from the free morpheme *go*. Which other words in the text are formed from the same morpheme? How are they related to the theme of the narrative?
2. Examine the morpheme/word *begin* in the same way in the narrative.
3. *She sat in an **unaccustomed** part of the theatre with him*

    How many morphemes make up the adjective *unaccustomed*?
    Which free morpheme are they based around?
    Why does Joyce choose this adjective? (Why not, for example, the short near synonym <u>strange</u>?)
4. Can you identify any other multi-morphemic adjectives in the narrative? How and why do they draw attention?

Exploring & Writing

Task A
Work in a group of three.

1. Each person thinks of a theme for a short narrative (e.g. based on an incident, a recollection, a moment of epiphany, or one of contemplation or indecision). Each person then makes a list of the nouns needed to write the first paragraph of the narrative.
2. Show your list to the other members of your group to see if they can guess the theme of your narrative.
3. Select one of the themes and its list of nouns. Each person chooses one of the lexical categories below and notes the words needed:

---

[1] Hudson, R. (1994). 'About 37% of Word-Tokens are Nouns'. *Language,* 70 (2), 331–339.

verbs
adjectives
adverbs

4. Work as a group to write the paragraph using the 4 lists.

Task B

Choose 3 short stories with which you are familiar. Without looking at the stories, predict the balance of lexical category use in the first paragraph of each.

Task C

1. Write your own opening paragraph for a narrative of a genre of your own choice (e.g. romance, thriller, mystery, fantasy). Decide which lexical category you have most used and delete all the examples of this category. Pass your narrative to other members of the group.
2. Identify the missing lexical category in the narrative you receive. Try to fill in the missing words.
3. Return the narrative to its writer and discuss using the ideas from this chapter.

Task D

1. Re-write your text so it has more nouns than verbs or more verbs than nouns.
2. Add adjectives to your nouns and adverbs to your verbs.
3. What effects do these transformations have?

Review & Reflection

Task A

1. Work with a partner to recall the meanings.

    Free morpheme
    Bound morpheme

2. Match the 8 main lexical categories with their functions.

Lexical category	Function & example
Nouns	Words which describe nouns e.g. *dusty*
Verbs	Words which join phrases, clauses and sentences e.g. *and*
Adjectives	Names for people, places, things & states e.g. *man*
Adverbs	Words which can take the place of nouns e.g. *she*
Determiners	Words which state actions, events and states e.g. *look*
Prepositions	Words which come before nouns to specify which noun e.g. *the*
Pronouns	Words which describe verbs e.g. *usually*
Conjunctions	Words which describe how something relates to a noun e.g. *at*

Task B

1. Identify the lexical categories in the following sentence:

   But in her new home, in a distant unknown country, it would not be like that.

2. Which items belong to open categories and which to closed?

Task C

Comment on the proportions of nouns, adjectives and verbs you would expect to find in the following types of text:

- Legal document
- Publicity material on a bottle of shampoo
- Newspaper website report of a football match

Chapter 3
Nouns and Noun Phrases

In Essence

In this chapter you explore the structure and use of noun phrases in Joyce's *Eveline*. You consider how Joyce uses noun phrases to construct the narrative and introduce multiple perspectives. You then build on these ideas to explore use of noun phrases in your own writing.

Check the Basics

In Chap. 1, we referred to words and phrases as two units of analysis (alongside others). Now let's examine what this means by focussing on nouns and noun phrases. A **noun**, as we saw in Chap. 2, is a **lexical category**. A **noun phrase** is a larger unit of analysis that depends on (and must include) a noun; other elements are optional. It is a **syntactic category,** that is, an identifiable pattern that explains how English structure is organised.

One main **function** of a noun phrase is as the **subject** of the sentence. The subject is normally placed in the beginning of the sentence and signifies the person or thing involved in the action expressed by the verb, usually as the agent of the action. Noun phrases also function as **objects**. The object follows the verb and stands for the person or thing also involved in the action, but either as the goal, or recipient, or beneficiary. We'll explore these relationships further in Chap. 7.

The tables below illustrate the forms of noun phrases used in the narrative.

In the first table the examples have two noun phrases (as subjects and objects).

Noun phrase used as subject	Verb	Noun phrase used as object
Her father	*had found out*	*the affair*
The boat	*blew*	*a long mournful whistle*

© The Author(s), under exclusive license to Springer Nature Switzerland AG 2022
S. Lavender, S. Varella, *Grammar in Literature*,
https://doi.org/10.1007/978-3-030-98893-7_3

In the second table of examples the subjects are fulfilled by pronouns. As we said in Chap. 2, pronouns replace nouns; they may therefore function as subjects or objects, occupying the 'slot' of the noun phrase.

Pronoun used as subject	Verb	Noun phrase used as object
I	*know*	*these sailor chaps*
She	*was about to explore*	*another life with Frank*

In the examples in the third table there are no objects, but the examples have **prepositional phrases**. These are phrases that depend on (and must begin with) a preposition (underlined), followed by a noun phrase..

Noun phrase used as subject	Verb	Prepositional phrase
The evening	*deepened*	<u>*in*</u> *the avenue*
The man out of the last house	*passed*	<u>*on*</u> *his way home*

All noun phrases have a **head noun** which is the main focus of the phrase. Hence *father* is the head noun of *her father*, *chaps* is the head noun of *the sailor chaps* and *man* is the head noun of *the **man** out of the last house*.

The table below shows how noun phrases allow more information to be added to the head noun. Information placed before the head noun is called **premodification**. This is often a determiner followed by one or more adjective(s) or a noun whose **function** coincides with that of an adjective, i.e. it is used to describe or specify the head noun.

Premodification		Head noun
Determiner	Adjective(s)/ noun(s)	
The	*sailor* (n)	*chaps*
His	*blackthorn* (n)	*stick*
A	*long mournful* (adj. + adj.)	*whistle*

As in the tables below, information can also be placed after the head noun and is called **postmodification**.

Premodification	Head noun	Postmodification
The pitiful	*vision*	*of her mother's life*
The invariable	*squabble*	*for money*

Occasionally, postmodification can also be carried out by adjective(s).

		Postmodification
Determiner	Head noun	Adjective(s)
Her	*cheeks*	*pale and cold*

Textual Analysis of the Narrative

In the two examples below, **prepositional phrases** are used to postmodify the head nouns..

Determiner	Head noun	Postmodification Prepositional phrase
The	names	of the ships
The	white	of two letters

Another common form of **postmodification** of noun phrases is by **complement clauses** as in the table below. We will look in more detail at complement clauses later in the book (in Chaps. 8 and 9), but for now it suffices to say that complement clauses begin with the **complementizers** *that* and *who, whom, whose, which, of which*, etc. (traditionally known as **relative pronouns**) and identify or give more information about the noun they modify.

Premodification	Head noun	Postmodification with a complement clause
The two young	children	who had been left to her charge
The	lass	that loves a sailor

Many of the noun phrases in the narrative are heavily premodified and postmodified; quite often both simultaneously as in the table below.

Premodification Determiner + adjective	Head noun	Postmodification Prepositional phrase
A sudden	impulse	of terror
An unaccustomed	part	of the theatre

One final feature of noun phrases in the narrative is the use of **noun phrases in apposition**. This is where a noun phrase follows another, both having identical reference. One example of this is *she, Eveline*.

Textual Analysis of the Narrative

Task A

1. Identify the head noun in each of the following noun phrases.

    the odour of dusty cretonne
    the man out of the last house
    a man from Belfast
    the children of the avenue
    the name of the priest

2. How is the postmodification in each of the phrases similar?

Task B

1. What is similar about the following noun phrases?

   the concrete pavement
   the cinder path
   the new red houses
   their little brown houses
   bright brick houses
   shining roofs

2. These phrases all occur at the beginning of the narrative. What are the effects of the use of these similar phrases?

Task C

1. What are the head nouns in the following phrases? What is similar about the structures of the phrases?

   its familiar objects which she had dusted once a week for so many years
   those familiar objects from which she had never dreamed of being divided
   the name of the priest whose yellowing photograph hung on the wall above the broken harmonium beside the coloured print of the promises made to Blessed Margaret Mary Alacoque

   What effects do their structures create?
2. Identify the head noun in the following sentence.

   He would save her.

   Comment on the contrast with the noun phrases in 1 above.

Task D

1. Joyce repeats the noun phrase *the odour of dusty cretonne*. Identify both occurrences. What effects does the repetition have?
2. Twice in the narrative we find Eveline sitting by the window. Identify the noun phrases used to describe her exact position. What significance do the phrases have?
3. How does Joyce use 'black' in the narrative as a premodifying adjective?
4. Many of the other premodifying adjectives or nouns in the noun phrases have negative connotations, e.g. *melancholy, pitiful, dark*. Find two further examples. What are the cumulative effects?
5. The noun phrases:

   a hard life
   a wholly undesirable life
   another life

   appear in quick succession. Find the phrases in the narrative. What is similar about their structures? What effects does the repetition have?

Task E

1. Towards the end of the narrative, several of the noun phrases have a similar structure.

   All the seas of the world
   A cry of anguish
   No sign of love or farewell or recognition

   Identify the structure. What are the effects?
2. Read the paragraph beginning *'She stood among the swaying crowd...'* (the scene at the docks) and identify all the noun phrases, (regardless of their positions in the sentences).
   What effects does noun phrase modification have in this paragraph?
3. Identify and comment on the use of the word 'sea/seas' in noun phrases in the narrative.

Exploring & Writing

Task A

1. Think of your own past. Think of three important events; e.g. start of university, eighteenth birthday, house move. (Make sure they are all noun phrases.)

   Take three strips of paper and write one event in the centre of each strip as in the example below. (Don't show the strips to anyone!)

   birth

2. Write a premodification and then a postmodification for the noun on each strip as below.

   The highly unexpected **birth** of my delightful baby sister

3. Fold each strip so the head noun is hidden. Show the folded strips to a partner or small group. Can you guess the missing head nouns?

Task B

1. Work as a group. Choose one of the nouns below to use as a head noun and build the longest (meaningful!) noun phrase you can using both pre and postmodification.

cat   tomato   love   sorrow   acupuncture

Compare your phrases.
2. What do you see as the natural limits on the length of the written noun phrase?

Task C

1. You plan to write the opening paragraph of a narrative about a moment of indecision. Decide what the indecision is and choose a setting (scene) which reflects the indecision.
2. Write an opening sentence for your narrative which consists only of a head noun and a verb phrase.
3. Explain your ideas for your paragraph to a partner and pass your writing to the partner.
4. Use the ideas your partner has explained to add premodification and postmodification to the noun phrase in the writing you receive.
5. Then rework the same noun phrase into a parallel noun phrase in a slightly different format and note this on the paper (e.g. *a street organ playing* and *the organ player*).
6. Pass the work back to the first writer.
7. Continue your paragraph and work in the second noun phrase.
8. Read your paragraph to your partner and/or group and comment particularly on the use of the noun phrases.

Task D
Choose another short narrative and identify the use of noun phrases used as significant motifs throughout the narrative.

Review & Reflection

Task A
Using the name 'Eveline' as a head noun, create a noun phrase with both premodification and postmodification which reflects your view of the character in Joyce's narrative.

Task B
Listen to those created by other members of your group. Do any change or challenge your own understanding of the character?

Task C

In the early stages of writing, children in primary education are often encouraged to enrich their writing with pre and postmodification. What do you see as some of the pitfalls in the examples below?

The black and white stripy zebra walked across the green grass in the hot heat of the African sun.

I went to a party where I met a woman whose daughter knows my mother who you saw the day when we met where we usually go.

What advice would you give?

Task D

What thoughts has this chapter given you about the use of noun phrases in creative writing? Share your ideas.

Chapter 4
Verbs 1: Tense and Aspect

In Essence

In this chapter, the first of three on the richness of verbs, you explore the tenses and aspects of the verbs in *Eveline*. You consider particularly how Joyce uses verbs to sequence the narrative and to introduce multiple perspectives. You also explore some of the potentials of verbs in your own writing. (We also include a first note on 'mood' in relation to verbs.) The end of the chapter encourages you to explore some of the potentials of verbs in your own writing.

Check the Basics

In this chapter and Chap. 5 we focus on the **lexical category** of **verbs**. Chap. 6 moves us on to the next level of analysis, the **syntactic category** of **verb phrases**. You will have noticed the pattern by now: like nouns project onto noun phrases, verbs project onto verb phrases. This type of hierarchical structure is called phrase structure, or constituent structure. A **constituent** is a distinct syntactic unit within the overall structure of a sentence; e.g. the noun phrase *This grammar book* in the sentence *This grammar book is helpful.*

Noun and verb phrases are the most important syntactic categories at the level of the phrase, for reasons we explain in Chap. 7. Following that, you will gain a better understanding of the role of constituency, a notion that will become very useful as you progress in your study of theoretical grammar (See Chap. 1.)

For now, let's focus on verbs and their characteristics.

Tense

Verbs usually show time; i.e. they indicate when something happens. This is known as **tense**.

Simple present tense	*Everything **changes***
	*I **know** these sailor chaps*
Simple past tense	*She **sat** at the window*
	*Few people **passed***
Past perfect tense	*The waters **had gone** back*
(usually indicates something happened before something else)	*She **had dusted** once a week*

Note that some verb forms are not marked for tense, and they can never serve as the only verb forms in a sentence. Consider the following:

*She **sat** at the window <u>watching</u> the evening <u>invade</u> the avenue.*

Here, 'sat' is marked for tense and, in principle, can work alone in a sentence; 'watching' is a **participle**; 'invade' is an **infinitive**. Participles and infinitives are called **non-finite** (or tense-less) verbs. We return to participles and infinitives in Chap. 9. For now, you need to be able to simply distinguish them: participles end in -ing, while infinitives are sometimes preceded by 'to'; neither of them is marked for tense; in other words, their morphology is always fixed.

Aspect

Apart from tense, verbs can also indicate whether an action or state is complete or ongoing. This is known as **aspect**. The aspect of a verb can be simple, continuous, perfect. **Continuous aspect** is sometimes also referred to as **progressive aspect**. The term '**perfect**' is used to mean perfected or completed. Compare:

Tense and aspect of verb	Examples from the narrative
Present **simple** (habitual)	*He **is** in Melbourne now*
	*Don't you **see**?*
	*I **know** these sailor chaps*
Present **continuous** (ongoing)	*These ladies **are waiting***
Past **simple** (completed)	*She **heard** his footsteps*
	*She **looked** round the room*
	*He **showed** the photograph*
Past **continuous** (ongoing)	*He **was lodging***
	*He **was standing***
	*They **were courting***
Past **perfect** (completed)	*The Waters **had gone** back to England*
	*All its familiar objects which she **had dusted** once a week*
	*Those familiar objects from which she **had** never **dreamed** of being divided*

In summary then, verbs can show both tense (past or present) and aspect (simple, continuous or perfect). The perfective features of aspect can also be combined with the simple or continuous aspects so that a verb can be, for example, past perfect continuous, e.g. he had been thinking.

(Note English does not have a future tense. There are many ways to indicate futurity in English, among them uses of modal and semi-modal verbs which we explore further in Chap. 5.)

A Note on Mood

The forms of verbs are indicative of what is called **mood**, a functional distinction which in this book we examine under Sentences (Chap. 10). Moods can be **declarative, interrogative or imperative**.

Declarative forms state information. They can be positive (sometimes also known as **affirmative**) or **negative**.

The verb form may also indicate a question (**interrogative**) or a command or request (**imperative**).

See the examples from the narrative in the table below.

Declarative (affirmative)	He **is** in Melbourne
	She **had** shelter and food
Declarative (negative)	Her father **was not** so bad
	She **would not cry** many tears
Interrogative	**Was** that wise?
	Do(n't) (= do + not) you see...?
Imperative	**Look** lively [!]
	Come(!)

Finally, in the examples of the formation of tense, aspect and mood above, you will notice that verbs make use of 'helping verbs'. These are known as **auxiliary verbs** and are underlined in the examples below. The **main verb**, that is, the lexical verb is shown in bold. For analysis purposes, we consider the formation auxiliary + main verb as the verb in a phrase or sentence.

Don't (= do + not) *you* **see** *these ladies are waiting? (mood)*
She <u>had</u> **dusted** *(tense)*
They <u>were</u> **courting** *(aspect)*

The verbs do/did, have/had, am/is/are/was/were are all used as auxiliary verbs.

Textual Analysis of the Narrative

Task A

Underline the verbs in each example below from near the beginning of the narrative.

One time there used to be a field there
They used to play every evening with other people's children

Then a man from Belfast bought the field and built houses in it
Her father used often to hunt them in out of the field
Now she was going to go away like the others

Task B
1. Comment on the following examples in terms of the use of *now* and verb tenses. When is *now* in the narrative?

   Now she was going to go away
   He is in Melbourne now
   Even now, though she was over nineteen

2. What is the tense of most of the verbs in the second paragraph?
3. Which verbs are in a different tense in the same paragraph?
4. Why do you think these verbs are in a different tense?

Task C
1. How does Joyce use tense to contrast the voice of the narrator with direct speech throughout the narrative?
2. What effects does this contrast have?

Task D
1. *She looked round the room, reviewing all its familiar objects which she had dusted once a week for so many years*

   What are the tenses and aspects of the verbs in this sentence? What is the effect of the contrast?
2. Find three other examples in the narrative of verbs with the same tense and aspect as above. What are the cumulative effects of their use?

Task E
1. What is the tense of the first verb in the example below?
   If she went, tomorrow she would be on the sea with Frank.
   Why is this tense used?
2. What do you notice about the verb tenses in the sentence
   It was hard work—a hard life—but now that she was about to leave it she did not find it a wholly undesirable life.
3. Can you find other examples of this technique in the narrative? What effects does it have?

Task F
1. Comment on the use of tense and aspect in the third paragraph, (the scene where Eveline looks around the room).
2. The narrative is narrated in the past tense. How do we still get a sense of the order of events, or the progression of time?
3. What other words help set the narrative in the past? Which lexical category do they belong to?

Task G

1. Most of the sentences in the narrative are declarative affirmatives. Find examples of interrogatives (questions) e.g. 'Was that wise?'. Who are the questions asked of?
2. Find three examples of imperatives (direct commands or requests) in the narrative. Who are they addressed to?
3. What effects do you think Joyce creates with these features?

Exploring & Writing

Task A

1. Use the ideas in the five boxes below (in any order) to form a narrative.

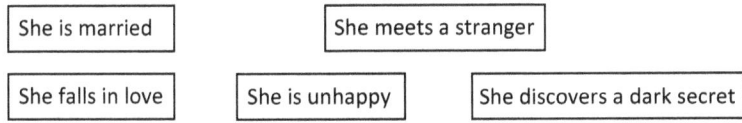

2. Work with a partner and compare your versions. Can you create any other versions? Choose the most interesting version.
3. Use this version to write the narrative together as a single paragraph using past tense verbs. You may add other ideas to the narrative if you wish.
4. Can you change the tense of any of the verbs to the present?
   Try changing the aspect of some of the verbs by making them continuous (e.g. is/was doing) and/or perfected (e.g. has/had done).
5. Compare and discuss the versions: which works better and why?
6. Read your preferred version to your group.

Task B

1. Choose a significant event in your own past. Draw 5 circles on a paper and complete each circle with the instructions in 2 below.
2. Circle 1: note the event.
   Circle 2: note a related date or time and a place.
   Circle 3: note a comment about the event and add the name of the person who could make this comment.
   Circle 4: note something which happened before the event.
   Circle 5: note an outcome of the event.
3. Pass your notes to a partner. Write about your partner's event using the notes you receive. You should include all the information in the circles. You can include the information in any order.
4. Read your versions to each other. Together review any inaccuracies and make improvements to the texts where you can.

5. Pass your versions to another group. Add an interrogative and an imperative to the versions you receive.
6. Work in a group of 4 to discuss the effects with the original writers.
7. Review and improve your own original text and read it again to the group.
8. Discuss what you have learnt about verbs.

Task C

Choose another short narrative with which you are familiar. Note the tenses and aspects of the verbs in its first main paragraph. Compare your notes with use of tenses and aspects in the final main paragraph in the same narrative. Point out any interesting features.

Review & Reflection

Task A

Underline the verbs in the following sentence.
Ernest had been her favourite but she liked Harry too.
What tenses are they in and why do you think the tenses are different? Which are the main verbs?

Task B

Complete the table below to show how the verb in the sentence 'Everything changes' could be adapted by the use of different tenses and aspects.

	Simple	Continuous/progressive	Perfect	Perfect continuous/progressive
Present	changes			has been changing
Past		was changing	had changed	

Why do you think Joyce chooses the present simple form for the narrative?

Task C

Verbs are sometimes called the most essential word of a text as they alone can form a single regular sentence (e.g. *Escape!*) without the addition of other elements. As you have worked through this chapter, what has struck you most about the roles of verbs in Joyce's and other narratives?

Chapter 5
Verbs 2: Modality, Catenation and Multi-Word Verbs

In Essence

This second chapter on verbs builds on the previous one to explore Joyce's uses of verb tones (modality). The chapter also considers how verb forms can be chained (or catenated) to other verb forms and how they can link with prepositions and adverbs to form multi-word verbs of compound meanings. These devices are considered particularly in terms of the introduction of doubt and views from multiple perspectives in the narrative. The Exploring & Writing activities then encourage you to bring together your insights from this unit and Chap. 4.

Check the Basics

Please note this chapter assumes you have already worked through Chap. 4 and are familiar with its terminology.

Modality
Modal verbs such as *can, could, must, would* combine with main verbs (lexical verbs) to add a lens through which an action or state (expressed by the main verb) is viewed. Like auxiliaries, they always precede the main verb, which is why they are also called modal auxiliaries. In analysis, the formation modal + main verb is considered as the verb of a phrase or clause.

Consider:

Subject	Modal verb	Main verb	Object	Modal 'lens' adds ...
She	*could*	hear	*a street organ*	**ability**
She	*must*	escape		**necessity**
Frank	*would*	save	*her*	**possibility and/or willingness**

Verbs can also include **semi-modal verbs** such as *used to, have to* and **marginal modal auxiliaries** such as *be going to* and *be about to*. These also add a lens in a similar way to the modal verbs above. Consider the examples below.

Subject	Semi-modal or marginal modal	Main verb	Object/ adverbial	Modal 'lens' adds ...
He	*used to*	call	*her (Poppens)*	**repetition of past action**
She	*had to*	rush	*out*	**obligation**
She	*was going to*	go	*away*	**(future) intention**
She	*was about to*	leave	*it*	**(future) immediate action**

We explore some effects of the modals, semi-modals and marginal modals in the narrative in the textual analysis section.

Catenation

Catenation means 'chaining'. It refers to the way, as in some of the examples above, verb forms can link with other verb forms to combine, semantically, two different actions. Here are some further examples from the narrative.

*She **wanted to live***
*They **seemed to have been** rather happy then*
*He **had begun to threaten** her*
*She **continued to sit** by the window*

These verbs are another important feature of the narrative which we also explore further in our analysis of the text.

Multi-Word Verbs

Sometimes a main verb can be composed of more than one word; e.g. *They **found out** that she had run away*. In this case the verb *found* and the adverb *out* are combined to create a compound meaning of 'discovered'. In other words, the meaning is not simply the result of the addition of its constituent parts.

Other examples from the narrative include:

*Her time was **running out** (expiring)*
*He had never **gone for** her (attacked)*

As the examples show, multi-word verbs are formed from a lexical verb with an adverb (example 1) or preposition (example 2). (The main difference is that a preposition is followed by a noun phrase as in the first example where *for* is the preposition and *her* is the object noun phrase.) Often, again as in the examples, multi-word verbs are used in place of a single verb which has a similar meaning. We also explore some of the effects of this in the analysis below.

Textual Analysis of the Narrative

Task A
1. Many of the verbs in the narrative include the modal *would*. It is used to express a range of meanings. What meaning 'lenses' does *would* add to the verbs in the following examples?

   *Perhaps she **would** never **see** again those familiar objects*
   *She **would not cry** many tears at leaving the Stores*
   *She **would not be treated** as her mother had been*
   *In the end he **would give** her the money*
   *Frank **would save** her*

   Do you think any of the phrases express more than one meaning of 'would'?
2. What effects does Joyce create with the repeated use of the modal *would* in the paragraph beginning '*But in her new home, in a distant unknown country...*'?
3. Match the meanings of the modal 'lenses' in the following examples.

Examples	Meaning of the modal lens
She ***must*** *escape*!	Possibility
Could she still *draw back* (after all he had done for her?)	Ability
Her promise to keep the home together as long as she ***could***	Duty
He ***would*** *save* her	Necessity
Why ***should*** she *be* unhappy?	Willingness

This exercise is not straightforward. Why?

4. Look again at the paragraph beginning *But in her new home, in a distant unknown country....* Experiment with the modality by adding modal verbs from the table above. What effects can you create?

Task B
1. From the phrase *One time there used to be a field* ... the text becomes dense with repeated use of the semi-modal 'used to'. What meanings does this emphasize? What effects does the repeated use create?

2. In the examples of *used to* below, two of the subjects are the father and two are Frank. Which are which?

> *(He) **used to** pass it with a casual word*
> *He **used to** meet her outside the Stores every evening*
> *He **used to** call her Poppens*
> *(He) often **used to** hunt them in*

What lens of meaning does 'used to' add to the verbs?

Why does Joyce cause Evelyn to use the same semi-modal to reflect on the actions of the two men, one she has known all her life and one she has met recently?

Task C

1. Comment on Joyce's use of the marginal modal 'be about to'.
   She was about to leave it
   She was about to explore another life
2. Comment on the use of the marginal modal 'be going to'.
   She was going to go away
   He said he wasn't going to give her his hard-earned money
3. What roles do you think these semi-modals have in the development of the narrative?

Task D

1. Indicate the catenated verbs in the examples below.

   i. *She continued to sit by the window*
   ii. *He took her to see the Bohemian Girl*
   iii. *But she wanted to live*
   iv. *She was to go away with him by the night boat to be his wife and to live with him in Buenos Ayres*
   v. *They had come to know each other*
   vi. *Still they seemed to have been rather happy then*
   vii. *Her father ... had forbidden her to have anything to say to him*

2. This is a narrative about a potential new beginning. What are the effects of catenation following the uses of 'begin' in the examples below?

   > Latterly he *had begun to threaten* her
   > The invariable squabble for money on Saturday nights *had begun to weary* her
   > Then she *had begun to like* him

3. How does Joyce use catenation to connect the characters in the narrative?
4. How does Joyce use modality and catenation to reflect the complexity of Eveline's decision?

Task E

1. Joyce makes use of several multi-word verbs in the narrative. Match each of the multi-word verb uses with a single lexical verb in the table below.

Examples with multi-word verbs in italics	One-word lexical matches
The Waters *had **gone back*** to England	Take
They found out that she *had **run away*** with a fellow	Withdraw
Her place *would be **filled up*** by advertisement	Escape
He *had* never ***gone for*** her	Expire
He ***read*** her ***out*** a ghost story	Return
Her time *was **running out***	Attack
Could she still ***draw back*** after all he had done for her?	Read

2. Locate each example in the text. What would be the overall effect of replacing the multi-word verbs with single word verbs? Why does Joyce use the multi-word forms?

Exploring & Writing

Task A
1. Write two statements about your past life. Each one should be a complete sentence. They do not need to be true.
2. Pass your statements to another member of the group. Add one of each of the following to each of the sentences you receive. You can use them to indicate whether or not you believe each statement.

   Modal verb
   Catenative verb

3. Read your sentences to the group and comment as necessary.

Task B
1. With a partner choose a well-known fairy tale. Tell each other the story.
2. Write the story together as a single paragraph. Make sure each person has their own copy of the paragraph.
3. Here are the verb forms we have explored in this chapter.

   Modal verbs (e.g. *will/would, can/could, should, must*)
   Semi & marginal modal verbs (e.g. *used to, be going to, have to, be about to, happen to*)
   Catenative verbs (e.g. *want to, seem to, begin to, continue to*)
   Multi-word verbs (e.g. *run out, go for*)

   Work on your own version of the story to work in at least one example of each of the above forms. (You can include any you already have!)
4. Read your paragraphs to each other. Comment on aspects you think work or do not work. In what ways do your choices influence the tone of the story?

Task C
1. Work together to rewrite your narrative from the perspective of one of its protagonists. You can do this directly or you can use Joyce's method of giving an indirect voice to the character.
2. Read your completed versions to the group and discuss any points you find interesting.

Review & Reflection

Task A
This task helps you to review the terminology from Chap. 4 and this chapter. Work with a partner to match the nine terms with the examples from the narrative in the table below.

Term	Example
Single word verb: past simple declarative	*Don't (you) see?*
Verb with an auxiliary verb to form past perfect simple	*Was about to leave (it)*
Verb with an auxiliary verb to form past continuous	*had (shelter and food)*
Interrogative verb (present simple)	*Must escape*
Single word verb: imperative	*found out*
Verb with modal verb	*had dusted*
Verb with semi-modal	*come!*
Verb with catenation	*were courting*
Verb with past simple multi-word verb	*continued to sit*

Task B
Work in a group of 3 or 4 people for this task. Each group needs a die. (Please make sure you cannot view Task A.)

Take turns from right to left to roll the die. The number on the die selects a row from the chart below. Choose one of the terms in the row and give examples and/or a definition of the term. If your group members think you are correct you win the point. If you cannot answer, the turn passes to the person on your left. Cross out each cell as the group answers it. If the row you select has already been crossed out you miss your turn. Add up your points at the end! (Use Task A to check any terms you are still unsure of.)

1	Simple present verb	Verb with a modal
2	Present perfect verb	Verb with a multi-word verb
3	Verb with catenation	Simple past verb

Review & Reflection

4	Imperative verb	Past continuous verb
5	Past perfect verb	Verb with a semi-modal
6	Interrogative verb	Past perfect continuous verb

Task C
1. Which aspects of Chaps. 4 and this chapter have been new to you?
2. Which aspects do you consider most significant to Joyce's narrative?

Chapter 6
Verb Phrases

In Essence

In this chapter we explore the structure and use of verb phrases in Joyce's *Eveline*. You develop your understanding of verbs from Chaps. 4 and 5 to consider how Joyce uses verb phrases (including complements and adjuncts) to construct the narrative and establish relationships between characters, events or states of being, objects and situations. You then build on these ideas to explore the use of verb phrases in your own writing.

Check the Basics

In Chaps. 4 and 5 we focus on the **lexical category** of **verbs**. In the current chapter we move on to the next level of analysis, the **syntactic category** of **verb phrases**. As we said at the beginning of Chap. 4, as nouns project onto noun phrases, so verbs project onto verb phrases. Noun phrases and verb phrases are distinct **constituents** of English sentence structure. Below we examine the structure of verb phrases. The following Chap. 7 then moves us to a yet further level of analysis (that is, from a smaller to a larger constituent, or from **phrase** to **clause**), which will demonstrate why noun and verb phrases are the most important syntactic categories at the level of the phrase.

For now, let's focus on verb phrases.

A **verb phrase** is a larger unit of analysis that depends on (and must include) its equivalent smaller unit of analysis, in other words, a verb; other elements are optional. **Verb phrase** is a **syntactic category,** that is, a constituent, an identifiable and common pattern of English structure.

The **head** of the verb phrase is therefore a **verb**. It is the most central element in the phrase upon which other (optional) elements depend.

At the very least, the verb phrase can consist of only a verb as in the examples below.

(Few people) passed.
(Everything) changes.

In addition to the verb, verb phrases may also include **complements** and **adjuncts** of the verb.

Complements can be noun phrases which depend entirely on the verb that directly precedes them. In this case they function as the object(s) of that verb.

*(She) would not cry **many tears** at leaving the Stores.*

Adjuncts are usually adverbs or adverbials (larger units that behave like adverbs) that may follow the verb and its complement(s). They add more information about the circumstances in which the event signified by the verb takes place.

*(She) would not cry many tears **at leaving the Stores**.*

In what follows below, we examine complements and adjuncts closely, looking at the processes of transitivity and the use of adverbials in verb phrases.

Transitivity
Verbs followed by a **direct object** are called **transitive verbs** (that is, the verb transitions between a subject and its object). The action undertaken by the subject thus implicates something or somebody else (the object).

Noun phrase	Verb phrase	
Subject	Verb	Direct object
A man from Belfast	bought	the field
She	would never see	those familiar objects
She	had never found out	the name of the priest

A few verbs can relate to two objects, one **direct** and another **indirect**; these are called **ditransitive verbs.**

Noun phrase	Verb phrase			
Subject	Verb	(Indirect) Object	(Direct) Object	(Indirect) Object
He	would give	her	the money	
He	showed		the photograph	to a visitor

As indicated in the table above, indirect objects express the recipient or the beneficiary of the action of the verb. When they are expressed by a pronoun, e.g. *her*, they are often placed before the direct object. Hence the first example above could also be written as 'He would give the money to her'.

Not all actions, of course, impact on somebody or something else. In this case the verb phrase is composed of an **intransitive** verb, as in examples we started the section with.

(Few people) passed.
(Everything) changes.

Copular Verbs

Certain verbs are followed by a **complement**, which describes or refers to the subject (or sometimes the object) in a clause. You may thus prefer to use the terms **subject** and **object complement**, to distinguish them from the more general category of complements, i.e. noun phrases following the verb as direct or indirect objects.

The verbs taking a subject or object complement are known as **copular verbs.**

Common copular verbs are *to be, to become, to feel, to seem, to appear, to look, to call/be called, to be named.*

The table below shows examples from the narrative with a **subject complement**.

Noun phrase	Verb phrase	
Subject	Copular verb	Subject complement
Her father	*was*	*not so bad*
Her mother	*was*	*alive*
They	*seemed to have been*	*rather happy*
She	*felt*	*elated*

The table below shows an example with an **object complement**.

Noun phrase	Verb phrase		
Subject	Copular verb	Object	Object complement
He	*used to call*	*her*	*Poppens*

Adverbials

An **adverbial** is a group of words used in place of a single adverb, and also provide information about the place, time, manner, reason, etc. of the action expressed by the clause.

Eveline begins *She sat at the window.* Here, *she* is a noun phrase, *sat at the window* is a verb phrase; *at the window* is a **prepositional phrase** (a category first introduced in Chap. 3 and examined in relation to noun phrases), which does the same job as an adverb; hence the convenient term 'adverbial'. The adverbial gives more information about the verb. Here it describes where she sat. (One way to identify an adverbial is to see if it can be replaced by a lexical adverb. Here the word 'there' could replace *at the window*.) The table below shows two examples from the narrative with adverbials which denote place.

Noun phrase	Verb phrase	
Subject	Verb	Adverbial
She	*sat*	*at the window*
The evening	*deepened*	*in the avenue*

Adverbials usually give more information about when, where, how or why an action or state takes place. See the further examples of adverbials from the narrative in the table below.

Example	Noun phrase	Verb phrase		
	Subject	Verb	Adverbial(s)	Function of adverbial(s)
1		*Look*	*lively*	Manner
2	*The man out of the last house*	*passed*	*on his way home*	Place
3	*The two children…*	*went*	*to school regularly*	Place + Frequency
4	*They … all*	*had … gone*	*for a picnic to the hill of Howth*	Reason/purpose + Place

Please note the following points about elements that may be considered adverbials.

- Example 1 shows they can consist of just a single adverb.
- Example 2 shows a prepositional phrase. Other examples from the narrative are: *The children of the avenue used to play together <u>in that field</u>; She had to work hard <u>both in the house and at business</u>* (two prepositional phrases joined up).
- Examples 3 and 4 show two adverbials in combination.

Also note that adverbials of time and place often occur at the end of a clause. They can, however, also occur at the beginning as in the examples below.

But <u>in her new home in a distant unknown country</u> it would not be like that (place)

<u>During all those years</u> she had never found out the name of the priest (time)

Textual Analysis of the Narrative

Task A
Work with a partner. The examples below all come from paragraph 7 of the narrative.

He _____ she used to squander the money
It _____ hard work
Then she _____ to rush out
In the end he would _____ her the money

Textual Analysis of the Narrative 45

1. From memory, fill in the missing verbs and then order the phrases as they occur in the narrative.
2. Identify an example from 1 above of each of the following.

   A transitive verb
   A ditransitive verb
   An intransitive verb
   A copular verb

3. Without looking at the text, add verb phrases to the subject noun phrases from the same paragraph. (You can use any words you wish to make appropriate verb phrases.)

   People
   Ernest
   Harry

4. Compare your answers with your group and with the text.
5. Discuss the relationship between the meanings of the verbs and the meanings of their complements.

Task B
1. Here are nine examples of copular verb phrases from the narrative in the order they occur. Decide, in each case, who the subject is (Eveline, her father or Frank).

   ----- *was tired*
   ------ *was not so bad then*
   ------ *would be married*
   ----- *was usually fairly bad on Saturday night*
   ------ *was very kind, manly, open-hearted*
   ------ *felt elated as she sat in an unaccustomed part of the theatre*
   ------ *was awfully fond of music*
   ------ *was becoming old lately*
   ------ *could be very nice*

2. Note the complements of the verbs for each of the characters. What patterns can you identify?
3. How are the characters presented differently (via the use of copular verb phrases) at different points in the narrative?
4. Identify the copular verb phrases in the examples below. What effects do they cumulatively create?

   That was a long time ago; she and her brothers and sisters were all grown up her mother was dead.
   Ernest was dead and Harry, who was in the church decorating business, was nearly always down somewhere in the country.
   The station was full of soldiers with brown baggages.

5. Identify another example from the narrative to support your observations.

Task C

1. The following examples from the narrative have transitive and ditransitive verbs which involve Eveline, her father and Frank in subject and object positions. Identify the subject and object(s) in each case.

   he had never gone for her
   he would give her the money
   he took her to see the Bohemian Girl
   he would save her
   he held her hand
   he had done for her
   he would drown her

2. Discuss the meaning and transitivity of the verbs in relation to who is involved in the action.
3. What do you notice about Eveline? What do you notice about the father and Frank?
4. Identify two further examples from the narrative to support your observations.

Task D

Joyce makes significant use of adverbials in the narrative.

1. From the eight examples below, identify the adverbials, e.g. of place, time, etc.
   In her home anyway she had shelter and food
   she had dusted once a week for so many years
   During all those years she had never found out the name of the priest
   She stood up in a sudden impulse of terror
   Through the wide doors of the sheds she caught a glimpse
   The boat blew a long mournful whistle into the mist
   He rushed beyond the barrier

2. Which of the adverbials are in unusual positions? Why do you think this is?
3. At the beginning of the narrative Joyce often uses adverbials at the end of clauses, for example:

   Her head was leaned <u>against the window curtains</u>
   She heard his footsteps clacking <u>along the concrete pavement</u>
   The children of the avenue used to play together <u>in that field</u>
   Her father often used to hunt them <u>out in the field</u>

   Why do you think this is? What effects does he create?

4. Towards the end of the narrative, there are also a number of similar clauses which have adverbials of place. How do they contrast with those at the beginning?

   The boat blew a long mournful whistle <u>into the mist</u>
   Her distress awoke a nausea <u>in her body</u>

Exploring & Writing

> *A bell clanged <u>upon her heart</u>*
> *All the saes of the world tumbled <u>about her heart</u>*
> *He rushed <u>beyond the barrier</u>*

What is the contrast?

Task E
1. Some of the adverbials above are quite long. What do you think their length adds to the narrative?
2. *She heard his footsteps clacking <u>along the concrete pavement</u> and afterwards crunching <u>on the cinder path before the new red houses</u>*
   In the sentence above the adverbials of place are underlined. What are the effects of Joyce's use of two adverbials of place in the same sentence?
3. Which sections of the narrative are densest in terms of the frequency of adverbials of time and place? Why and what effects does Joyce create?

Exploring & Writing

Task A
1. Choose one of the clauses below to work with.

   they met secretly
   we have been planting acorns
   the frog was catching flies

2. Add a time adverbial to the beginning of the clause and then add an adverbial of place to the end of the clause to make a complete sentence.
3. Pass your sentence to another member of the group. Do one of the following (in the order they appear) and then pass the resulting sentence on to a different member of your group each time.

   i. Add an adverb of frequency (e.g. often, rarely) to the time adverbial.
   ii. Add an adverb of intensity (e.g. quite, fairly) to the time adverbial.
   iii. Add more information to the adverbial of place.
   iv. Add an adverbial of manner.
   v. Add an adverbial expressing purpose (e.g. to …).
   vi. If you can, move the position of any of the adverbial phrases in the sentence.

4. Return the sentence to the original writer. Read out the final sentences. What are the effects of lengthening the adverbials? Can the original sentences 'support' all the inserted ideas?
5. Are there any limits on how long the adverbials can be? What natural limits do you think 'work' in a written text?

Task B

1. Here are the four sentences of the final short paragraph of the narrative. Work alone and rework the sentences to include the changes outlined below each sentence. You should try to maintain the sense of the original narrative.

    i. *He rushed beyond the barrier and called to her to follow.*
        Change the adverbial of place.
    ii. *He was shouted at to go on but he still called to her.*
        Make the verb in the second verb phrase ditransitive.
    iii. *She set her white face to him, passive, like a helpless animal.*
        Change the verb.
    iv. *Her eyes gave him no sign of love or farewell or recognition.*
        Change the verb from ditransitive to transitive.
2. Compare your new version of the paragraph with a partner. Discuss the use of verb phrases and adverbials.

Task C

1. Write a short paragraph of at least 4 sentences about yourself, using only copular verbs.
2. Now continue your text with another paragraph of at least 4 sentences (still about yourself), using only transitive and ditransitive verbs.
3. Read the resulting texts to your group.
4. What differences of foci do you notice between the paragraphs? What conclusions can you draw?

Review & Reflection

Task A
Work with a partner.

1. From the excerpt below identify one example of each of the following.

    A copular verb
    A transitive verb
    A ditransitive verb
    An adverbial describing pace
    An adverbial referring to time

    Home! She looked round the room, reviewing all its familiar objects which she had dusted once a week for so many years, wondering where on earth all the dust came from. Perhaps she would never see again those familiar objects from which she had never dreamed of being divided. And yet during all those years she had never found out the name of the priest whose yellowing photograph hung on the wall above the broken harmonium beside the coloured print of the promises made to Blessed Margaret Mary Alacoque. He had been a school friend of her father. Whenever he showed the photograph to a visitor her father used to pass it with a casual word:

2. Recall the types of complements and adjuncts explored in this chapter.
3. What do you consider the most important information you have learnt from the chapter?

Task B

Discuss in a group.

Which features of verbs explored in this chapter do you find most significant in the construction of Joyce's narrative? Why?

Chapter 7
Basic Clauses

In Essence

In this chapter you explore how noun phrases and verb phrases combine to create clauses, which are the essential building blocks of sentences. You examine the set of formulations a basic clause can have and prepare yourself for a closer examination of Joyce's sentences. As usual, the chapter concludes by inviting you to explore your own creative use of clauses.

Check the Basics

Having highlighted the importance of noun and verb phrases in Chaps. 3 and 6 respectively, in this chapter we move to the next level of analysis, the clause. Put simply, a **basic clause** is a noun phrase followed by a verb phrase. A clause is a constituent, a separate identifiable unit that may be included in a larger unit. Below we examine how we can identify clauses as constituents.

All clauses are formed of a **subject** and a **predicate**. As in the table below, the subject is usually the topic of the sentence and the predicate normally gives information about the state of the subject, about what the subject does or about what happens to the subject.

Examples of basic clauses are shown below.

Basic clause	
Subject	Predicate
She	sat at the window
Her head	was leaned against the window curtains
She	was tired

© The Author(s), under exclusive license to Springer Nature
Switzerland AG 2022
S. Lavender, S. Varella, *Grammar in Literature*,
https://doi.org/10.1007/978-3-030-98893-7_7

Basic clause	
Subject	Predicate
Few people	*passed*
A man from Belfast	*bought the field*
The children of the avenue	*used to play together in that field*

As the examples show, the subject is always a noun phrase; the predicate is always a verb phrase. You should be able to identify subjects and predicates fairly easily, so long as you remember the elements of the noun phrase (head noun plus any pre- or postmodifiers) and the elements of the verb phrase, which we examined in the previous chapter but also remind you of below.

Predicates always follow subjects and can have 7 basic forms as shown in the table below. For clarity here, we present a simple complete narrative with two characters, Jane and Matthew.

Example	Subject	Predicate	Example
1	S +	Verb	Jane/ arrived
2	S +	Verb + Object	Matthew/ watched/ Jane
3	S +	Verb + Complement	Matthew/ felt/ happy
4	S +	Verb + Adverbial	Matthew/ moved/ quickly
5	S +	Verb + Object (indirect) + Object (direct)	Jane/ gave/ Matthew/ a stroke
6	S +	Verb + Object + Complement	Matthew/ made/ Jane/ happy
7	S +	Verb + Object + Adverbial	Jane/ put/ Matthew's food/ in the cat bowl

Textual Analysis of the Narrative

Task A

1. In the clauses below identify the subjects and their predicates.

    It was hard work
    The evening deepened in the avenue
    Her distress awoke a nausea in her body

2. Match each of the subjects with their predicates from the final part of the narrative and complete the missing verbs. (Try to do this without looking at the narrative!)

Subject	Predicate
She	_____ *the iron in frenzy*
All the seas of the world	_____ *him no sign of love or farewell or recognition*
Her hands	_____ *among the swaying crowd in the station at the North Wall*
Her eyes	_____ *about her heart*

Textual Analysis of the Narrative 53

3. *Through the wide doors of the sheds she caught a glimpse of the black mass of the boat*

   What is the subject of this clause?
   What is the predicate?
   Identify another clause in the narrative with a similar structure.
   What effects does Joyce create by placing the subject later in the clauses?

Task B

1. The following 3 sentences each have only one clause and have the same structure. What is the clause structure? (Hint: use the table in the 'Check the basics' section to help you.)

   He is in Melbourne now.
   The evening deepened in the avenue.
   A bell clanged upon her heart.

2. Which 2 of the following sentences have the same clause structure? What is the structure?

   She knew the air.
   Frank would save her.
   Their passage had been booked.

   What are the effects of the use of this (simple) structure?

Task C

1. Underline the complements in the following examples. In each case, note if they are complements of the subject, direct object or indirect object.

   i. *That was a long time ago; she and her brothers and sisters were all grown up her mother was dead.*
   ii. *It was hard work—a hard life—but now that she was about to leave it she did not find it a wholly undesirable life.*
   iii. *The station was full of soldiers with brown baggages.*

2. There is a sense in which the complement in the penultimate sentence of the narrative could apply simultaneously to the subject, direct object and indirect object.

   She set her white face to him, passive, like a helpless animal.

   Identify the complement and explain this point. Do you agree?

Task D

1. The following sentences also contain only one clause. Match the examples to the clause structures. (Use the table in 'Check the basics'.)

   i. *She was tired.*
   ii. *Everything changes.*
   iii. *She stood up in a sudden impulse of terror.*
   iv. *He would save her.*

v. *The station was full of soldiers with brown baggages.*
vi. *She answered nothing.*
vii. *The boat blew a long mournful whistle into the mist.*
viii. *Her hands clutched the iron in frenzy.*

2. Which part of the narrative has the greatest concentration of sentences with a single clause? Why do you think this is? What effects does Joyce create?

Exploring & Writing

Task A
1. Work with a partner. Look back at the mini narrative about Matthew the cat in 'Check the basics'. Choose your own subject, perhaps a topical event or a well-known narrative. Write about your subject using only 7 clauses, one of each clause type as in the example. (You can use the 7 clause structures in any order.)
2. Exchange your narrative with another pair. Identify the clause structures in the narrative you receive.

Task B
1. In both the following opening lines, the first sentences consist only of a single clause. Why do you think they work? Do they share any features? What structures do the clauses have?

    'Ships at a distance have every man's wish on board.'
    Their Eyes Were Watching God, Zora Neale Hurston (1937)
    'All stories are love stories.'
    Eureka Street, Robert McLiam Wilson (1996)

2. Use one of the subjects below to write your own single clause opening sentence for an imagined novel or short story.
    Our heroine   The visitor   Dust   The facemask
3. Share your ideas with your group. Choose the best.

Task C
1. Select a paragraph of at least 10 lines towards the beginning of a short narrative you enjoy. Identify at least 4 of the clause structures. Are there any sentences composed of a single clause? How do these features make the paragraph 'work'?
2. Compare a paragraph towards the end of the same narrative. Are there any parallel or contrasted features?
3. If possible, look at the use of clause structure in something you have written yourself. Have you gained any insights about your writing which come from your exploration of clause structures in this chapter?

Task D

1. It has been argued[1] that Joyce's heroine's name might originate in *Eveleen's Bower*, a poem by Irish writer and poet Thomas Moore (1779–1852).
2. Read the poem (below). What's the story? (Hint: It's based on a Celtic myth.) Do you think the poem could be the basis for Joyce's narrative?
3. Work with a partner. Convert the final two stanzas of the poem to prose in modern English. You need to make any necessary changes so as to have regular, complete clauses.
4. Identify the clause structures you have used.
5. Compare your version with those of others in your group. Which version do you think best expresses the poem? Consider how the clauses help build the narrative.
6. Work with your original partner again. Discuss the choices you made together in terms of clause structures. Now you have heard all the versions from your group, would you make any changes to your own version?

Eveleen's Bower
Oh! weep for the hour,
When to Eveleen's bower,
The Lord of the Valley with false vows came;
The moon hid her light,
From the heavens that night,
And wept behind her clouds o'er the maiden's shame.

The clouds pass'd soon
From the chaste cold moon,
And heaven smiled again with her vestal flame;
But none will see the day,
When the clouds shall pass away,
Which that dark hour left upon Eveleen's fame.

The white snow lay
On the narrow path—way,
When the Lord of the Valley cross'd over the moor;
And many a deep print
On the white snow's tint
Show'd the track of his footstep to Eveleen's door.

The next sun's ray
Soon melted away
Every trace on the path where the false Lord came;
But there's a light above,
Which alone can remove
That stain upon the snow of fair Eveleen's fame.

---

[1] Florio, J. (1993) "Joyce's 'Eveline'". *Explicator*, Vol. 51, No. 3, pp. 181–184.

Review & Reflection

Task A

Work with a partner. Recall the 7 basic clause structures covered in this chapter.

Task B

1. Without looking at the text, which clause structures do you think Joyce uses most in the text?
2. Justify and discuss your answers. (Then see the answer section!)

Chapter 8
Sentences

In Essence

In this chapter you explore ways in which clauses can be combined to create sentences of more than one clause. You also explore the variety of sentence types in Joyce's narrative. At the end of the chapter you consider the effects of sentence types in your own and other authors' work.

Check the Basics

Once you have a clause, you have a sentence. A sentence made up of only one clause is called a **simple sentence**.
 For example:
 Few people passed. (1 clause = 1 event)
 The man out of the last house passed on his way home. (1 clause = 1 event)
 Combinations of clauses can be used to create longer sentences. See the examples of two-clause sentences in the table below.

Example	Sentence with 2 clauses	Sentence type
1	Then a man from Belfast _bought_ the field and [he] _built_ houses in it. (2 clauses = 2 events)	compound
2	Tizzie Dunn _was_ dead, too, and the Waters _had gone_ back to England. (2 clauses = 2 events)	compound
3	Whenever he _showed_ the photograph to a visitor her father _used to pass_ it with a casual word. (2 clauses = 2 events)	complex
4	Even now, though she _was_ over nineteen, she sometimes _felt_ herself in danger of her father's violence. (2 clauses = 2 events)	complex

© The Author(s), under exclusive license to Springer Nature
Switzerland AG 2022
S. Lavender, S. Varella, *Grammar in Literature*,
https://doi.org/10.1007/978-3-030-98893-7_8

As noted, the sentences in the table above contain two clauses each but there is an important difference in the way the clauses within them are structurally connected.

Examples 1 and 2 show clauses joined together by 'and', a **coordinating conjunction,** or simply **conjunction**. This combination of clauses is called **coordination** and the sentence created is a **compound sentence**. In compound sentences each clause can stand on its own. In other words, both clauses are **main** or **independent clauses**.

Compound sentences include the following coordinating conjunctions between their clauses.

and, or, but, for, nor, yet, so

Sentences 3 and 4 in the box above have a different structure as they have clauses separated by commas, and one of the clauses is introduced by a **subordinating conjunction** or **subordinator**. This combination of clauses is called **subordination** and the sentence created is a **complex sentence**. In a complex sentence one clause depends (both structurally and for its meaning) on the other. In other words, a **subordinate** or **dependent** clause introduces (or follows) a main or independent clause: *Though she was over nineteen, she sometimes felt herself in danger of her father's violence.* Here, the main clause (*she sometimes felt herself in danger of her father's violence*) could stand alone but the subordinate clause (*Though she was over nineteen*) needs to be anchored by the main clause.

Subordinating conjunctions include the following examples and are grouped here by their meanings.

- Time = *after, as, as soon as, before, once, since, until, when and whenever, while*
- Place = *where, wherever*
- Reason = *as, because, since*
- Comparison = *as, as if, as though, than*
- Condition = *as long as, if, in case, provided, provided that*
- Negative condition = *if ... not, unless*
- Concession = *although, as long as, even if, even though, though, whereas, while*
- Purpose = *to, in order to, so that*
- Result = *so that, so ... that, such ... that*

As you can see, subordination does much more than listing events in the order they take place. It explains, points to a point in time and space, creates contrast, etc. Subordinate clauses are often referred to as **adverbial clauses,** given the semantic notions they may express (time, place, etc.). In other words, their semantic roles in relation to their main clauses are similar to the semantic roles of adverbials in a clause.

It is important to note that the subordinate clause can precede or follow the main clause as in the examples below (with their subordinate clauses underlined).

<u>Though she was over nineteen</u>, she sometimes felt herself in danger of her father's violence.

Joyce could have written: She sometimes felt herself in danger of her father's violence, <u>though she was over nineteen</u>.

To give a further example, Joyce wrote_: As she mused_ the pitiful vision of her mother's life laid its spell on the very quick of her being; but he could have written The pitiful vision of her mother's life laid its spell on the very quick of her being _as she mused_.

Complement clauses (introduced already as a type of noun modification in Chap. 3) are similar to dependent clauses in that they contain a verb phrase but cannot stand alone. Their function is to modify a noun, hence the more specific term **noun-complement clause**.

For example:

And yet during all those years she had never found out the name of the priest whose yellowing photograph hung on the wall above the broken harmonium beside the coloured print of the promises made to Blessed Margaret Mary Alacoque.

In this sentence, the complement clause _whose yellowing photograph hung on the wall..._ modifies the noun 'priest'.

Common **complementizers** are _that, which, who, whoever, whom_ and _whose_.

The second role of complement clauses is to complement a verb. In this role, they are called **verb-complement clauses**. For example:

she knew that he was speaking to her... Here the complement clause _that he was speaking to her_ acts as a complement of the verb _knew_.

We explore complement clauses in more detail in Chap. 9.

Sentences can contain both compound and complex clauses. In this case, the sentences are described as **compound/complex sentences** as in the example below.

Not long before, when she had been laid up for a day, he had read her out a ghost story and made toast for her at the fire.

This sentence can be analysed as shown below.

Adverbial	Dependent clause	Independent clause and coordinate clause	Coordinate clause
Not long before	_when she had been laid up for a day_	_he had read her out a ghost story_	_and [he had] made toast for her at the fire_

Finally, and as in the example above, compound and complex sentences can contain **ellipsis.** This means that some elements are omitted or **ellipted** because their meaning is already clear by being carried over from the preceding elements. Here, then, Joyce does not need to repeat 'he had' in the final coordinate clause. We revisit ellipsis and its effects on the narrative in Chap. 9.

Textual Analysis of the Narrative

Task A
1. Match each of the examples below to a sentence type: simple, compound or complex. Then note the types of clauses in each sentence:

i. *Her time was running out but she continued to sit by the window.*
   ii. *She remembered the last night of her mother's illness.*
   iii. *As she mused the pitiful vision of her mother's life laid its spell on the very quick of her being.*

2. Identify another example of each type of construction in the narrative.

Task B
1. Now concentrate on your examples of compound sentences. What is their purpose? How are the events represented related to each other? In other words, is the sentence a sequence of events, or a contrast of events and/or situations?
2. Now concentrate on your examples of complex sentences. What is their purpose? How are the events represented related to each other? In other words, consider here how the narrative is built upon qualifications of time and place, cause and reason, result and consequence, as well as contrast, concession or adversative factors.

Task C
1. Look at the paragraph beginning *But in her new home....* There are four instances of 'but' in the paragraph, but not all of them are used as we have discussed previously in this chapter. Explore the sentences that include 'but'. What do you think? Is Joyce 'ungrammatical'? What effects does the repetition of *but* have?
2. Consider the sentence *What would they say of her in the Stores when they found out that she had run away with a fellow?'* How many clauses are there in this sentence? Identify the complement clause.
3. Consider the sentence *'People knew that they were courting and, when he sang about thee lass that loves a sailor, she always felt pleasantly confused.'* How many clauses are there in this sentence? Identify the complement clauses. What do you notice?

Task D
1. Examine the first paragraph of *Eveline* and consider Joyce's use of sentence structure. How does Joyce use contrasting structures to build the narrative?
2. Compare the first paragraph with the last (in terms of clause and sentence structure). What do you notice?
3. The narrative has some simple (and very short) sentences.

   He is in Melbourne now.
   Miss Gavan would be glad.
   She must escape!
   Frank would save her.

   Find two more examples of simple sentences in the narrative. At what points do these occur? How are they used? What is the contrast?
4. The description of Eveline's life with Frank and his previous life uses many compound sentences, e.g.

   He was awfully fond of music and (he) sang a little.

He had sailed through the Straits of Magellan and he told her stories of the terrible Patagonians.

How does this contrast with the description of Eveline's life with her father? What are the effects of the contrast?

Exploring & Writing

Task A
1. Work in a group of 3 or 4. Use the simple sentence:

    Sarah loved Peter.

    Take turns to choose a conjunction from the box below

---

and – until – after – but – although – so – because – yet – whenever

---

2. Write a compound or complex sentence each time which includes the simple sentence and the given conjunction (without showing your group members).
3. Read and compare your sentences.
4. Agree which are compound and which are complex.
5. As a group choose 2 of the compound sentences and 2 of the complex sentences. Change the order of the clauses in each sentence. What are the effects? What do you notice?

Task B
1. The table below shows six well-known first sentences in novels. Match each opening sentence with its novel and author.

Opening sentence	Novel & author	Sentence type
It was a bright cold day in April, and the clocks were striking thirteen.	Pride & Prejudice Jane Austen (1813)	
Life changes fast.	Mrs Dalloway Virginia Woolf (1925)	
It is a truth universally acknowledged, that a single man in possession of a good fortune, must be in want of a wife.	The Great Gatsby F. Scott Fitzgerald (1925)	
As Gregor Samsa awoke one morning from uneasy dreams he found himself transformed in his bed into a gigantic insect.	Moby-Dick Herman Melville (1851)	
Mrs Dalloway said she would buy the flowers herself.	The Year of Magical Thinking Joan Didion (2005)	

Opening sentence	Novel & author	Sentence type
In my younger and more vulnerable years my father gave me some advice that I've been turning over in my mind ever since.	Metamorphosis Franz Kafka (1915)	
Call me Ishmael.	1984 George Orwell (1949)	

2. Identify the sentence types.
3. Why do the sentences 'work' as openings to their novels? How do they each draw the reader in?
4. Write your own first sentence to your novel of a lifetime. What type of sentence have you created? Share your ideas!

Task C
1. Use one idea from the story titles below to write a simple clause of the form S V OD.
   Our heroine   The visitor   Dust   The facemask
   Pass your clause to another person.
2. Develop the clause you receive into a compound sentence.
   Pass the sentence to another person.
3. Develop the sentence you receive into a compound/complex sentence.
   Pass the sentence to another person.
4. Develop the narrative by adding another simple sentence to develop the chronology of a story.
   Pass the text to another person.
5. Qualify the narrative by adding an adverbial clause to the last sentence.
   Pass the text back to its first author.
6. Read the versions to the whole group. What are the effects of the additions to the first clause?

Task D
1. Select one or two paragraphs from the beginning of a short narrative you enjoy. How are the sentences constructed? How does the writer use subordinate clauses? Look for both parallel structures and variation in sentence types and consider how these features make the paragraph 'work'.
2. Compare one or two paragraphs towards the end of the same text. Are there any parallel or contrasted features?
3. If possible, look at the sentences in something you have written yourself. Have you gained any insights about your writing which come from your exploration of sentences in this chapter?

Review & Reflection

Task A
1. Complete the following three sentences in your own words.

    Eveline is the heroine of the narrative but ...
    Eveline is the main protagonist of the narrative although ...
    Frank who ...

2. Which sentences are complex and which are compound? Why?
3. Read your sentences to your group. Which do you agree with?

Task B
Without complex sentences literature would be superficial and largely chronological.

How far do you agree with this statement? Explain your thinking to your group.

Chapter 9
Connecting Ideas: Clauses Revisited

In Essence

In this chapter you explore how Joyce combines the grammatical structures covered in previous chapters with additional forms to connect ideas, introduce new information and ultimately create his narrative. You examine complement clauses, direct and indirect speech, non-finite clauses, attenuation, ellipsis and 'dummy' subjects within clauses. You then consider how Joyce combines these elements to create layers and tones as he builds the narrative and frames its characters. As usual, the chapter concludes with opportunities for you to explore these features in your own writing.

Check the Basics

Complement Clauses
In Chap. 3 we looked at complement clauses as a form of postmodification in noun phrases; e.g. *a field in which they used to play every evening*.

Noun phrase		
Premodification	Head noun	Postmodification
a	field	in which they used to play every evening

The complement clause here thus gives more information about the head noun *field*. It is a dependent clause (see Chap. 8) introduced by complementizer (here *in which*) and, as a clause, it has its own verb phrase (here *used to play*).

© The Author(s), under exclusive license to Springer Nature
Switzerland AG 2022
S. Lavender, S. Varella, *Grammar in Literature*,
https://doi.org/10.1007/978-3-030-98893-7_9

The examples below show other complement clauses from the narrative with their complementizers highlighted. Complement clauses always modify a noun, independently of the position or function of the noun phrase.

Noun phrase		
Premodification	Head noun	Postmodification
A	house	(on the main road) **where** she used to visit
	Harry	**who** was in the church decorating business

In the table above, you will notice the two examples are slightly different in terms of grammatical construction. In the first, the complementizer *where* refers to the *house* which is the object of the complement clause. In the second, *who* refers to *Harry* who is the subject of the complement clause. When the complementizer refers to the object it can be omitted. So, Joyce could have written 'A house she used to visit'.

As we saw in Chap. 8, **complement clauses** may also complement the **verb**, as in the example below which contains a series of complement clauses:

> He <u>said</u> [that] she <u>used to squander</u> the money, that she <u>had</u> no head, that he <u>wasn't going to give</u> her his hard-earned money to throw about the streets.

Note [that] the complementizer 'that' may be omitted as described above.

Reported clauses are a sub-type of verb-complement clauses. In the example above, the sentence acts as a likely reported (sometimes known as **indirect**) version of the **direct statement** 'you used to squander money…'.

Non-finite Complement Clauses

In Chap. 4 we introduced non-finite verb forms. Non-finite verb forms are 'ing' and infinitive (with or without 'to') forms of verbs which are not marked for tense or aspect, e.g.

He had a home <u>waiting</u> for her
It had been an excitement for her <u>to have</u> a fellow

Non-finite complement clauses can be used to complement either the subject or the object in a clause.

Consider the following sentence:

She sat at the window <u>watching the evening invade the avenue</u>.

The *-ing* form here (*watching*) is a participle, and the underlined clause refers back to the subject *'she'*. It is a **subject complement** of the noun phrase *she*.

Now compare the sentence above with this sentence:

She heard his footsteps <u>clacking along the concrete pavement</u>.

Here, the underlined clause functions as an **object complement** of the noun phrase *footsteps* which is the object of the clause.

The same structure appears in the example below.

He had a home <u>waiting for her</u>.

The following example also includes an object complement, but the non-finite form is an infinitive.

She felt him <u>seize her hand</u>.

Infinitives may also be used to express purpose and, in this sense, can function similarly to adverbials.

Here are 2 examples from the narrative.

She had nobody <u>to protect</u> her
Her promise <u>to keep</u> the home together

In both cases, the infinitives act as postmodification to the nouns *nobody* and *her promise*.

In short, **complement clauses**, whether **finite or non-finite**, are used to add information about a lexical item. In a noun phrase, they modify a noun. Elsewhere in the clause, they act as complements to the subject or object (if non-finite clauses), or the verb (if finite clauses).

Copular Clauses

Copular clauses are those whose predicates are composed of copular verbs + complements, as in the examples below. Look back to Chap. 6 for a discussion of copular verbs.

Her mother was alive
They seemed to have been rather happy

Attenuation

In the second example above, the link between the subject and its complement is **attenuated** (or weakened) by the addition of *seem* to the verb phrase. This has both a lexical effect (i.e. *seem* introduces notions of uncertainty) but also has the effect of distancing the subject from the complement by the lengthening of the verb form. The clause *he could be very nice* shows a similar effect. (We explore this and other aspects of attenuation in this chapter.)

Ellipsis

We introduced the term **ellipsis** in Chap. 8. We noted that ellipsis occurs when some elements are omitted or **ellipted** because their meaning is already clear by being carried over from the preceding elements. This is shown in the example below.

Frank would take her in his arms, (and he would) *fold her in his arms.*

The full grammatical structure of the second clause is thus carried over from the first.

Dummy Subjects

As we have seen, all clauses (apart from those which are imperatives) need to have a subject. Sometimes a '**dummy subject**' can be used. Consider the following examples.

It was impossible.
One time there used to be a field there

In the first case, *it* refers to the impossibility of escape in a lexical sense. In a grammatical sense, though, there is no clear referent in the narrative for the pronoun *it*. In the second case, *there* introduces the lexical meaning of 'a field used to exist'. *There* operates in a similar way in the clause in the narrative *there were people listening*.

Textual Analysis of the Narrative

Task A

1. Fill in the missing complementizers (e.g. which, who etc.) in the examples from the narrative.

    i. *She knew it was that _____ had given her the palpitations*
    ii. *She had ... to see that the two young children _____ had been left to her charge went to school regularly and got their meals regularly*
    iii. *She was to go away with him ... to live with him in Buenos Ayres _____ he had a home waiting for her.*
    iv. *Another day, _____ their mother was alive*

2. Why does the following example not include a complementizer?

    He told her the names of the ships he had been on

3. Identify the complement clause in the following sentence.

    And yet during all those years she had never found out the name of the priest whose yellowing photograph hung on the wall above the broken harmonium beside the coloured print of the promises made to blessed Margaret Mary Alacoque

    What is unusual about the sentence?

Task B

1. The narrative has the following examples of reported speech.

    He said she used to squander the money, that she had no head, that he wasn't going to give her his hard-earned money to throw about the streets

Textual Analysis of the Narrative 69

> *He would ask her ... if she had any intention of buying Sunday's dinner*
> *He had fallen on his feet in Buenos Ayres, he said, and had come over to the old country just for a holiday*

What is different about the structure of the third example?

2. The narrative also contains the following 7 examples of direct speech.

> *"Miss Hill, don't you see these ladies are waiting?"*
> *"Look lively, Miss Hill, please"*
> *"I know these sailor chaps" he said*
> *She remembered her father strutting back into the sickroom saying "Dammed Italians! coming over here!"*
> *... her mother's voice saying constantly with foolish insistence "DerevaunSeraun! DerevaunSeraun!"*
> *"Come!"*
> *"Eveline! Evvy!"*

Suggest why Joyce chooses direct speech for the latter examples and reported speech for the former (in 1 above).

Task C

1. Identify the non-finite complement clauses below. All refer to Eveline, describing her actions. The first one is done for you.
   She sat at the window <u>watching the evening invade the avenue</u>.

   i. *She looked round the room, reviewing all its familiar objects which she had dusted once a week for so many years, wondering where on earth all the dust came from.*
   ii. *Then she had to rush out as quickly as she could and do her marketing, holding her black leather purse tightly in her hand as she elbowed her way through the crowds and returning home late under her load of provisions.*
   iii. *Her time was running out but she continued to sit by the window, leaning her head against the window curtain, inhaling the odour of dusty cretonne.*
   iv. *She would be on the sea with Frank, steaming towards Buenos Ayres.*

2. Identify the non-finite complement clauses in the sentences below. Eveline is again the subject of each sentence, but the non-finite clauses relate to another person or object. Identify the noun phrase the complements relate to. The first one is done for you.
   She heard <u>his footsteps clacking along the concrete pavement</u> and afterwards <u>crunching on the cinder path before the new red houses</u>. (Footsteps: direct object)

   i. *She remembered her father putting on her mother's bonnet to make the children laugh.*
   ii. *Down far in the avenue she could hear a street organ playing.*
   iii. *She remembered her father strutting back into the sickroom saying: "Damned Italians! coming over here!"*

iv. *She heard again her mother's voice saying constantly with foolish insistence.*
v. *She caught a glimpse of the black mass of the boat, lying in beside the quay wall.*

Task D

1. In the Check the Basics section, we looked at two noun phrases postmodified by infinitives acting as adverbials of purpose.

   She had nobody <u>to protect</u> her
   Her promise <u>to keep</u> the home together

   The examples below also use infinitives of purpose (underlined).

   i. *The trouble was <u>to get</u> any money from her father*
   ii. *She remembered her father putting on her mother's bonnet <u>to make</u> the children laugh*
   iii. *She prayed to God <u>to show</u> her what was her duty*
   iv. *He ... called to her <u>to follow</u>*

   In what ways are they similar and/or different to the first examples?
2. Why is the narrative quite dense with adverbials of purpose?

Task E

1. Underline the six copular verb phrases in the clauses below.

   Her mother was dead
   That was a long time ago
   Everything changes
   She and her brothers and sisters were all grown up
   He had been a school friend of her father
   She had nobody to protect her
   Frank was very kind, manly, open-hearted
   She felt elated

2. The following clauses also contain copular verb phrases. In each case, the link between the noun phrase and its complement has been attenuated (weakened). How is this achieved?

   They seemed to have been rather happy then
   It seemed a few weeks ago
   Miss Gavan would be glad
   Then she would be married
   She sometimes felt herself in danger of her father's violence
   She always felt pleasantly confused

   What effects does Joyce create?

Task F
1. Identify ellipsis in the examples below.

   She would not be treated as her mother had been
   Harry always sent up what he could
   Her promise to keep the home together as long as she could
   What would they say of her in the Stores when they found out she had run away with a fellow? Say she was a fool perhaps ...

2. Insert any words which would be necessary if the examples were not ellipted.
3. Why do you think Joyce uses the ellipted versions?

Task G
1. In which of the following clauses beginning with *it* do you think *it* functions as a 'dummy' subject? (Hint: you need to view the clauses in their contexts to decide this!)

   it was hard work
   it seemed a few weeks ago
   it should come that very night to remind her of the promise to her mother
   it was impossible

2. What effects does Joyce create by beginning many of the sentences in the narrative with pronouns (it, he, she etc.)?

Exploring & Writing

Task A
1. Consider the pairs of sentences below. What are the differences in meaning in each pair?

   i. Weeping, she saw him.
      She saw him weeping.
   ii. Weeping, she touched him.
       She touched him weeping.
   iii. Shivering with fear, she found him.
        She found him shivering with fear.
   iv. Snoring, she heard him.
       She heard him snoring.
   v. Realising the truth she killed him.
      She killed him realising the truth.

2. Which sentences 'work'?
3. Does the '-ing' participle complement the subject or the object in each case?
4. How can a reader tell if the complement relates to the subject or the object of each clause?

Task B

1. Which of the examples below 'work' for you?

    i. Expecting a reply to her message, the computer was always on.
    ii. Sally, no emails arriving in her inbox, waited in vain.
    iii. Pacing around the room in circles, she restarted the computer.
    iv. Feeling hopeless, she deleted the dating app.

2. What advice can you give about using 'ing' participles as subject and object complements?
3. Now check if your ideas fit the examples below.

    i. Being dull, he left the party.
    ii. Being dull, the party bored him
    iii. Pouring wine, he left the party.

Task C

1. Use ellipsis (and other methods) to shorten the sentence below as much as possible whilst retaining its meaning.

    Sally felt that if she had not heard of the app and if she had not decided to install the app she would never have put all her hopes on the app and she would never have been so unhappy.

    Compare your versions.
2. Does the example below 'work'? What are the issues?
    Sally would never have imagined she could fall in love, but then she did.

Task D

Think of an amusing, frightening or exciting event which has happened to you.

1. Briefly describe your event to your group.
2. Take brief notes on each event you hear.
3. Your tutor will give each person the name of one other member of your group.
4. Retell the event of your group member to the group as if you were a witness at the event (which has been described to you).
5. Think about the language you and group members used in task 4. What changes in language (from the version you originally heard) did task 4 call for?
6. Consider your own retelling in task 4. Which of the features from this chapter did you use?

Task E

1. Think of an event you have witnessed or heard about (this might be an incident at which you have been present or one someone has told you about).
2. Write a simple account of the incident in no more than three sentences.
3. Pass your account to a partner.
4. With the version you receive, carry out the following modifications.

    Attenuate at least one verb phrase e.g. by adding seem or a modal verb
    Add an example of direct speech

　　　　Add an example of reported speech
　　　　Add any other kind of complement clause, finite or non-finite
　　　　Add an adverbial of purpose (i.e. to …)
5. Return the work to the original writer and discuss the impact of the modifications.

Review & Reflection

Task A
Recall the main devices considered in this chapter which Joyce uses to interweave ideas in his narrative.

Task B
What advice would you give a writer about the use of 'ing' forms in subject and object complements?

Task C
Consider how the choice of grammar achieves a higher level of complexity with regard to the events, the characters and the objects involved.

Chapter 10
Framing and Compiling: Sentences and the Text

In Essence

In this chapter on framing and compiling the narrative, we use a whole-text approach to further explore Joyce's use of sentence types along with punctuation and paragraphing. We also pick up again on aspects considered in the early chapters of this book relating to lexical use, noun phrases and verb phrases, to examine their impacts at a text level. Taking this approach enables us to explore ways in which Joyce uses cumulative effects to weave images and echoes through the narrative. The chapter concludes by inviting you to explore a similar process in the work of Dickens and in your own writing.

Check the Basics

Sentence Moods

In Chap. 4 we saw that verb forms indicate the **mood of the sentence**, (**declarative, interrogative** or **imperative**). Sentences can thus be described as declarative, interrogative or imperative. As noted before, **declarative** sentences state information. (They are also sometimes called **indicative**.) They can be positive (sometimes also known as **affirmative**) or **negative.** Sentences can also pose questions (**interrogative**), give commands or requests (**imperative**), or express surprise or strong emotions (**exclamative**).

See the examples of sentences from the narrative in the table below.

| Declarative | She sat at the window watching the evening invade the avenue. |
| Interrogative | Miss Hill, don't you see these ladies are waiting? |

© The Author(s), under exclusive license to Springer Nature Switzerland AG 2022
S. Lavender, S. Varella, *Grammar in Literature*,
https://doi.org/10.1007/978-3-030-98893-7_10

Imperative	Look lively, Miss Hill, please.
	Come!
Exclamative	Home!
	Escape! She must escape!

At text level, you consider not only the form but also the distribution and frequency of each of these sentence moods across the text.

Passive Voice

When a clause has a transitive or ditransitive verb phrase it can also be written to 'front' the direct or indirect object. For example

He would give her the money could be written as:
She would be given the money.
    or
The money would be given to her.

This has the effect of giving importance or **prominence** to an object.

Examples of passive voice in the narrative include:

The organ player had been ordered to go away and given sixpence
Their passage had been booked

The subjects (underlined above) are thus the 'recipients' of the action of the verb phrase. Passive voice is often used to maintain focus or flow in a text by spotlighting the main interest, e.g. The youth stole the goods, but then (he) was arrested.
At text level, we relate the distribution of active and passive voice to the characters and consider the dynamics between them.

Minor Sentences

As we saw in Chaps. 6 and 7, sentences need to include at least a subject and a predicate (minimally, a verb); e.g. *Everything changes.*

Minor sentences do not fit this pattern. For example, in the narrative we find the following 5 minor sentences: *Home!, Escape!, No! No! No!* where each consist just of single words.
As in the table above, imperatives can consist of a single verb, and exclamatives can consist of just a noun or an interjection; in these cases they are both expressed as minor sentences.

Connectors: Conjunctions and Discourse Markers

As we saw in Chap. 2, conjunctions link words, phrases and clauses. Common conjunctions in the narrative are: *and, then, but, because* etc. which are used to create compound and complex sentences (see Chap. 7).

There is also a looser group of words and phrases which can be used to link sentences e.g.

But she wanted to live.
Then she had to rush out as quickly as she could...

These are usually known as **discourse markers** (sometimes just as 'connectors'). They stand outside the grammatical structures of the sentences they connect, but give 'flow' to the text, as in the examples, by referring back to previous ideas.

Discourse markers can also provide a comment which can stand apart from the main body of the text, e.g.

> <u>Of course</u>, her father had found out the affair and had forbidden her to have anything to say to him.

Discourse markers can also occur within sentences, but again stand outside the grammatical structure of the sentence, e.g.

> Say she was a fool, <u>perhaps</u>; and her place would be filled up by advertisement.

Punctuation

Punctuation refers to conventions of written text to convey or clarify meanings. Joyce's narrative makes use of the following widely used conventions:

- **capital letters** to begin sentences and for proper names;
- **full stops** to end sentences;
- **question marks** for questions;
- **exclamation marks** for imperatives and exclamatives;
- **commas** between listed items and to separate some clauses;
- **quotation marks** to indicate direct speech.

Joyce's narrative also makes use of the following features.

Punctuation	Name	Example	Comment
:	Colon	*He was drawing her into them: he would drown her.*	2 independent clauses with no coordinating conjunction and a contrast in meaning
;	Semi-colon	*She remembered the last night of her mother's illness; she was again in the close dark room at the other side of the hall*	2 independent clauses with no coordinating conjunction
—	dash	*Then she would be married—she, Eveline.*	An informal type of punctuation often used to create emphasis

Paragraph

Joyce's text is presented in paragraphs. A **paragraph** is generally accepted as a sentence or series of sentences related by a main theme.

Lexical Set

A **lexical set** is not a grammatical category, but rather a group of words linked by a common theme. For example, throughout the narrative, we find many examples of human-made spaces, openings and barriers e.g. *field, avenue, window, gate, railing.*

Stative & Dynamic Verbs

As noted in Chap. 4, verb phrases can express states and events. **Stative** verbs normally refer to thoughts or states of being e.g. believe, know, Iive. Examples from the narrative include:

She <u>had</u> nobody to protect her
She <u>knew</u> the air
She <u>felt</u> him seize her hand

Dynamic verbs normally express things which happen e.g. go, do, fall. Examples from the narrative include:

A man from Belfast <u>bought</u> the field and <u>built</u> houses in it
The children of the avenue used to <u>play</u> together in that field

Parallelisms

Parallelisms are repeated ideas or structures in a text. For example, several actions of both Eveline's father and Frank are described using *used to* in the verb form.

Her father <u>used</u> often <u>to</u> hunt them
He <u>used to</u> meet her outside the Stores every evening

Textual Analysis of the Narrative

Task A

1. Complete the phrase to make it true. Most of the sentences in the narrative are:

    Minor
    Simple
    Compound
    Complex
    Compound/complex

2. What effects does Joyce create by varying sentence constructions? What patterns can you identify?
3. Complete the phrase to make it true. Most of the sentences in the narrative are:

    Declarative
    Interrogative
    Imperative

4. What effects does Joyce create by varying sentence moods? What patterns can you identify?

Task B

1. The narrative has 5 examples of the use of passive voice:

    She would not be treated as her mother had been
    The two young children who had been left to her charge

Textual Analysis of the Narrative   79

The organ player had been ordered to go away and given sixpence
Their passage had been booked
He was shouted at to go on

The first example could be re-written as 'They would not treat her as they had treated her mother'. Re-work the other 4 examples using 'They' as a subject in each case.
2. What are the effects?
3. Look at each example in its context in the narrative. Try substituting the re-worked example. Discuss why they don't work so well in their contexts in the narrative.

Task C
1. Which of the following sentences do you consider minor sentences?

   i. *Home!*
   ii. *Say she was a fool, perhaps; and her place would be filled up by advertisement.*
   iii. *And yet during all those years she had never found out the name of the priest whose yellowing photograph hung on the wall above the broken harmonium beside the coloured print of the promises made to Blessed Margaret Mary Alacoque.*
   iv. *But in her new home, in a distant unknown country, it would not be like that.*
   v. *And now she had nobody to protect her.*
   vi. *Everything changes.*

2. Why do you think Joyce chooses to include minor sentences?

Task D
1. Identify the discourse markers in the following examples.

   Of course she had to work hard
   Of course, her father had found out about the affair
   In her home anyway she had shelter and food
   Her father was not so bad then; and besides, her mother was alive
   He would give her life, perhaps love, too

2. Whose 'voice' do the discourse markers portray?

Task E
1. The following three sentences all include use of a semi-colon.

   Her father was not so bad then; and besides, her mother was alive.
   That was a long time ago; she and her brothers and sisters were all grown up her mother was dead.
   She remembered the last night of her mother's illness; she was again in the close dark room at the other side of the hall and outside she heard a melancholy air of Italy.

   What effects does Joyce create?

2. Identify 2 more uses in the narrative. Are the effects similar?
3. In the following sentences Joyce uses dashes (−) as a form of punctuation.

   Then a man from Belfast bought the field and built houses in it—not like their little brown houses but bright brick houses with shining roofs.
   The children of the avenue used to play together in that field—the Devines, the Waters, the Dunns, little Keogh the cripple, she and her brothers and sisters.
   As she mused the pitiful vision of her mother's life laid its spell on the very quick of her being—that life of commonplace sacrifices closing in final craziness.

   Why do you think Joyce does this and what effects are created?
4. Identify 2 more uses of dashes in the narrative. Are the effects similar?
5. How many paragraphs does the narrative include? Can you identify the main topic of each paragraph?

Task F

1. Nouns of body parts occur frequently in the narrative:

   She felt him seize <u>her hand</u>
   Her <u>hands</u> clutched the iron in frenzy

   Identify 4 other uses of body parts (e.g. *cheek, face*). What are the cumulative effects?
2. Note all the noun phrases in the narrative which include the word *life*. What do you notice?
3. As mentioned before, nouns referring to human-made spaces, openings and barriers e.g. *field, avenue, window, gate, railing* also occur frequently. Identify 4 other items in the narrative which belong to the same lexical set. What are the effects?
4. Another reoccurring lexical set is that of sounds. Identify 4 items belonging to this set. Again, what are the effects?
5. What are the overall effects of Joyce's use of reoccurring images throughout the narrative?

Task G

1. Below is a list of clauses from the narrative with their subjects omitted. Identify the subject of each clause as Eveline, her father or Frank.

   heard his footsteps
   used to hunt them in out of the field
   had consented to go away
   had never found out the name of the priest
   had hard work to keep the house together
   took her to see the Bohemian Girl
   used to call her Poppens
   had sailed through the Straits of Magellan

> *had read her out a ghost story and made toast for her at the fire*
> *wanted to live*
> *stood among the swaying crowd*
> *caught a glimpse*
> *rushed beyond the barrier*
> *still called to her*

2. Look at the list again and divide the verb phrases into stative and dynamic.
3. To which characters does Joyce attribute mainly stative verbs and to which dynamic?
4. What are the cumulative effects of this division?

Task H
1. Several of Eveline's memories of Frank share a similar structure.

   > *He had started as a deck boy at a pound a month on a ship of the Allan Line going out to Canada.*
   > *He told her the names of the ships he had been on and the names of the different services.*
   > *He had sailed through the Straits of Magellan and he told her stories of the terrible Patagonians.*
   > *He had fallen on his feet in Buenos Ayres, he said, and had come over to the old country just for a holiday.*

   What is similar about the structures of the sentences? What effects does the repetition create?

2. As mentioned, several of the memories of Eveline's father and Frank also share structural similarities.

   > *Her father used often to hunt them in out of the field with his blackthorn stick.*
   > *her father used to pass it with a casual word*
   > *He said she used to squander the money*
   > *He used to meet her outside the Stores every evening*
   > *He used to call her Poppens out of fun.*

   What is similar about the structures of the sentences? What effects does the parallelism create?

3. Look at the following 10 descriptions of Eveline.

   > *She was going to go away like the others*
   > *She had consented to go away*
   > *She tried to weigh each side of the question*
   > *Now that she was about to leave it*
   > *She was about to explore another life with Frank*
   > *She was to go away with him by the night-boat to be his wife by the night-boat to be his wife and to live with him in Buenos Ayres*
   > *Then they had come to know each other*
   > *She had begun to like him*

Sometimes he could be very nice
If she went, tomorrow she would be on the sea with Frank

What devices does Joyce use in the verb forms to distance Eveline from her intended actions?

Are there any other ways within the narrative in which Joyce attenuates Eveline's resolve to change her life?

Exploring & Writing

Task A
Work with a partner.

1. Choose a section from Joyce's narrative of 1 or 2 paragraphs.
2. Note the salient structural features.
3. Together, and without looking at the narrative, try to recreate the text in Joyce's style from memory.
4. Compare your version with the original version.
5. Now rewrite the same section from Eveline's father's or Frank's perspectives. Again, try to write in the style of Joyce.
6. As a group, compare and discuss your texts.

Task B
1. As a group, choose a theme for a short narrative.
2. Outline 3 characters to participate in the narrative.
3. Decide the setting and outcome of the narrative.
4. Each person should now work alone to decide:

    a) A lexical set which can be used to develop an image to run through the narrative;

    b) The number of paragraphs needed to write the narrative.

5. Write an initial sentence to describe each of the 3 characters.
6. As a group, share and discuss your thoughts.

Task C
1. Here is the part of the text again from the opening of Charles Dickens' *Bleak House* which we considered in Chap. 1.

    Fog everywhere. Fog up the river, where it flows among green aits and meadows; fog down the river, where it rolls defiled among the tiers of shipping and the waterside pollutions of a great (and dirty) city. Fog on the Essex marshes, fog on the Kentish heights. Fog creeping into the cabooses of collier-brigs; fog lying out on the yards, and hovering in the rigging of great ships; fog drooping on the gunwales of barges and small boats. Fog in the eyes and throats of ancient Greenwich pensioners, wheezing by the firesides of their wards; fog in the stem and bowl of the afternoon pipe of the wrathful skipper, down in his close cabin; fog cruelly pinching the toes and fingers of his shivering little apprentice boy on deck. Chance people on the bridges peeping over the parapets into a nether sky of fog, with fog all round them, as if they were up in a balloon, and hanging in the misty clouds.

Imagine that Eveline is looking out over this scene from her window. Rework this paragraph in the style of Joyce (as used in the narrative) from Eveline's perspective.
2. Compare your paragraphs.
3. What does it mean to 'write in the style of' someone? Is it possible?

Review & Reflection

Task A
With a partner, check your understanding of the following metalanguage.

Declarative sentence
Minor sentence
Lexical set
Stative verb
Dynamic verb
Passive voice
Parallelism

Task B
Look back at the excerpt from *Bleak House* in Task C above. Find an example of each of the items above in Dickens' text.

Task C
Which features of Joyce's writing in Eveline do you think most important in constructing the picture of Eveline's desire yet inability to escape from her life?

Chapter 11
Bringing It All Together 1: A Holistic Review of Chaps. 2, 3, 4, 5, 6, 7, 8, 9 and 10 Based on Narrative 1

In Essence

Our final two chapters based on *Eveline* provide holistic overviews which bring together elements of Chaps. 2, 3, 4, 5, 6, 7, 8, 9 and 10. Chapter 11 reviews the grammatical structures covered so far and encourages you to explore how Joyce crafts his narrative in order to create the timeframe of events in the narrative, the links between people and objects as well as perceptions of Eveline's 'escape route'.

Check the Basics

This section is different from previous 'check the basics sessions' as our purpose is not to introduce new metalanguage and structures, but, rather, to provide a holistic overview of what has previously been covered. We begin with a brief overview.

As we have seen, at its most basic level, English syntax is quite simple.

- Words combine to make phrases.
- Phrases combine to make clauses.
- Clauses combine to make sentences.

In the previous Chapters we have looked at the most essential formations. Nouns form noun phrases and verbs verb phrases. A noun phrase in the subject position, followed by a predicate, a verb phrase, is the basic clause. Clauses can then be combined:

(a) two main clauses in a coordinated conjunction to create compound sentences;
(b) one dependent clause in a subordinated conjunction with a main clause to make up complex sentences.

Consider the sentence: *Few people passed.*

(Few) People = Noun with pre-modification
Passed = Verb
Few people passed = Noun Phrase + Verd Phrase = Clause = A Simple Sentence

We have also considered how this simple sentence could be developed:

Few people passed but they made a lot of noise. = A Compound Sentence (made up of two main clauses)
Even though the storm had cleared, *few people passed.* = A Complex Sentence (made up of a main and a subordinate clause)

In Chap. 2 we focused on **content words**, the lexical categories of nouns, verbs, adjectives and adverbs, the 'who-what-how-when-where' in the narrative. In Chaps. 3, 4, 5 and 6 we looked at **noun phrases** and **verb phrases**, the essential elements of the **clause**, which we examined in Chap. 7. In Chap. 8 we looked at how clauses combine to form larger **sentences**, while in Chap. 9 we looked at other ways to **connect ideas** and add detail and complexity. Chapter 10 examined other aspects of sentences, as well as features of the **text**.

Textual Analysis of the Narrative

The following tasks highlight and revisit the areas of analysis above and encourage you to view effects in terms of the whole narrative.

Task A

1. Eveline is introduced with the pronoun *she*. What effects does this introduction have? At what point does Joyce introduce the proper noun 'Eveline'? What effects does this have?
   What is the cumulative effect of the noun phrases *she* used as subjects?
2. Consider the use of the following noun phrases used as subjects throughout the narrative. What patterns do you notice?

   Her father
   Frank
   He

3. Frank is introduced thus: *She was about to explore another life with Frank.* What is the effect of introducing the character at the end of a prepositional phrase?
4. In the next sentence the proper noun '*Frank*' is immediately repeated as the subject of the sentence. Why is this?
5. Much of the next part of the narrative refers to Frank using the subject and object pronouns '*he*' and '*him*'. The next use of the proper noun is '*Frank would save her*'. Why?

Textual Analysis of the Narrative   87

6. Comment on Joyce's use of pronouns and possessives in the final four sentences of the narrative. What effects does the use create?
7. Several noun phrases in the narrative contain proper names e.g.
   People: *the Devines, the Waters, the Dunns, little Keogh the cripple*
   Blessed Margaret Mary Alacoque, Miss Gavan
   Places: *Belfast, Melbourne, Buenos Ayres*
   How do these contrast with the noun phrases in 2 above?
   What effects does the contrast have in the narrative?
8. In places, Joyce employs noun phrases with names of people in apposition e.g.

   she, Eveline
   little Keogh the cripple
   Eveline! Evvy!

   What are the effects of this?

Task B

1. When is 'now' in this narrative? How do you see the timeframe of the narrative?
2. Number the following events in chronological order.

   - Eveline sits in the window
   - Eveline meets Frank
   - Eveline plays in a field with children
   - Eveline's mother dies
   - Eveline does not leave with Frank
   - Eveline brings up her brothers
   - Ernest dies

3. Share your ideas: do you agree with others?
4. Comment on the tenses, aspects and moods in the verb phrases in the following examples. How do they presage the outcome of the narrative?

   Her head was leaned against the window curtains
   There used to be a field in which they used to play
   Now she was going to go away like the others
   If she went, tomorrow she would be on the sea with Frank
   He told her the names of the ships he had been on

Task C

1. Underline the examples of time adverbials in the clauses below.

   One time there used to be a field
   And yet during all those years she had never found out the name of the priest
   Then they had come to know each other
   One day he had quarrelled with Frank
   Now she was going to go away

2. Comment on the effects of the position of the adverbials.
3. Underline the examples of adverbials of place in the clauses below.

   In her home, anyway, she had shelter and food
   Down far in the avenue, she could hear a street organ playing
   Outside she heard a melancholy air of Italy
   Through the wide doors of the sheds she caught a glimpse of the black mass of the boat
   Amid the seas she sent a cry of anguish

4. Comment on the effects of the position of the adverbials.
5. How do other uses of time adverbials in the narrative contribute to the effect that the end of the narrative is inevitable from its beginning?

Task D

1. The noun phrase *the evening* appears both in the subject and in the object position in the narrative.

   *She sat at the window watching **the evening** invade the avenue*
   ***The evening** deepened in the avenue*

   What effects do the repetition and change of structure create?
2. Places and objects are very important in the narrative. What do you see as the significances of these places?

   - *The window*
   - *The field*
   - *Melbourne*
   - *Buenos Ayres*
   - *The dock*

3. And these objects?

   - *The stick*
   - *The black leather purse*
   - *The night-boat*
   - *The iron railing*
   - *The bell*

4. Choose one from each list above. Examine the structures of the sentences in which your selected place or object are first introduced. How do the structures relate the places and objects to the characters?
5. Eveline is ensnared by familiar places and objects, whilst at the same time yearning for the freedom she perceives in new places and objects.

   And yet during all those years she had never found out the name of the priest whose yellowing photograph hung on the wall above the broken harmonium beside the coloured print of the promises made to Blessed Margaret Mary Alacoque.

How does this sentence epitomise her ensnarement in the web of familiar places and objects?
6. Identify two other sentences which in their structures exemplify the same ensnarement in places and objects.
7. Contrast the above examples with:

> *Her hands clutched the iron in frenzy.*
> *She stood up in a sudden impulse of terror.*

8. How does Joyce's use of structure here emphasize Eveline's potential agency? What feelings do the sentences create?

> *Of course she had to work hard, both in the house and at business.*
> *Of course, her father had found out the affair and had forbidden her to have anything to say to him.*

Task E

Throughout the narrative Joyce weaves together complex sentences with complement clauses, short sentences of one clause, minor sentences and direct speech.

1. Identify one of each type in the examples below.

   > *She looked round the room, reviewing all its familiar objects which she had dusted once a week for so many years, wondering where on earth all the dust came from.*
   > *"He is in Melbourne now."*
   > *She was about to explore another life with Frank.*
   > *But she wanted to live.*

2. What effects do the two simple (i.e. one clause) sentences *She was tired* and *Few people passed* create at the beginning of the narrative?
3. Identify the sentence structures of *Escape! She must escape! Frank would save her.*
4. The first two sentences in 3 above are written as imperatives (i.e. commands). Who are the imperatives addressed to and who by?
5. *'Why should she be unhappy?'* Who produces this question and who is it addressed to?
6. Find two examples of direct speech in the narrative. Whose voices do they represent?

Task F

1. Number the examples in the order in which they occur in the narrative.

   > *Then she would be married – she, Eveline.*
   > *He said she used to squander the money*
   > *Of course, she had to work hard, both in the house and at the business*

> *Was that wise?*
> *Frank would save her.*
> *But now she was about to leave it she did not find it a wholly undesirable life.*
> *Miss Gavan would be glad.*
> *She must escape!*

2. Does Joyce write from the standpoint of an omniscient narrator? Which voices might be represented in the examples above?

Exploring & Writing

Task A
The tasks above have helped you review some of the metalanguage we have covered so far and consider how grammar works in the narrative. Below is a more complete list of key terms.

In a group, discuss how they are used in *Eveline*. Write down your thoughts. Can you cover them all? Read the answer section to check whether you agree.

> *nouns and noun phrases, verbs and verb phrases, stative and dynamic verbs, adjectives, pronouns, prepositional phrases, adverbials, aspect, tense, transitivity, modality, passive voice, basic clauses, complement clauses, embedding, non-finite clauses, 'dummy subject', statements, commands, questions, simple sentences, compound sentences, complex sentences, minor sentences, punctuation, sentence length, third-person narrative, viewpoint, direct speech*

Task B
Repeat Task A using a story you have written, or one you have read.

Review & Reflection

Task A
Preferably without looking at the terminology in the previous tasks, complete the table below, classifying the terms you remember according to the level of analysis they relate to. Note that a term may apply to more than one level of analysis.

Level of analysis				
Word	Phrase	Clause	Sentence	Text

Chapter 12
Bringing It All Together 2: A Holistic Appreciation of Narrative 1

In Essence

This final review chapter based on *Eveline* adopts a whole text approach to encourage appreciation of how Joyce crafts his narrative in order to create the timeframe of events in the narrative, the links between people and objects as well as perceptions of Eveline's 'escape route'. In this chapter we come closest to working with a holistic stylistic appreciation of the narrative.

Check the Basics

In this chapter we invite you to apply your knowledge and insight of grammar in a holistic way to the text. We take a different approach this time, attempting what is often called a top-down analysis, beginning with general aspects of the narrative and the text, and proceeding though sentence-level considerations down to lexical aspects. In other words, this is the reverse order from the one we have followed in Chaps. 2, 3, 4, 5, 6, 7, 8, 9 and 10, which started with smaller units and proceeded to larger units of analysis.

This approach allows us to further understand the contribution of grammar to textual analysis and narrative comprehension. The tasks below follow these steps:

- Approaching the narrative: initial questions
- Analysing the text: grammar and lexis
- Interpreting the text: meaning and effects

Textual Analysis of the Narrative

Task A
Work in small groups. Looking at *Eveline,* consider the following questions focussing on general aspects of narrative and the text:

1. What is this narrative about?

    i. What is the setting? What is the time and place?
    ii. Who are the main characters? Are there any secondary characters?
    iii. What do the characters do? What else happens?

2. Who is the narrative told by?

    i. Whose voice do you hear?
    ii. Are there any other voices represented?
    iii. Whose point of view is represented?

3. How is the narrative structured?

    i. Is the narrative chronological and linear?
    ii. Are there any points where the narrative structure and actual order of events differ from each other?

Task B
Work in small groups. Looking at *Eveline,* consider the following questions focussing on the text and its grammatical structures and lexis. You may want to annotate the text, or use highlighting, colour-coding, circling or underlining. These visual cues will help you assess the frequency and distribution of textual and grammatical features. As you consider each level of analysis below, look particularly for patterns and features which are common or repeated as well as for features which stand out because of their contrast or difference or absence.

1. How is the text structured?

    i. How many paragraphs are there?
    ii. How long are the paragraphs?
    iii. What is the transition between paragraphs?
    iv. Are there any interesting openers? Are there any noticeable expansion patterns, in other words, how do the paragraphs develop?
    v. Are there any interesting punctuation patterns?

2. What are the sentences like?

    i. Are they long or short?
    ii. Are they statements? Questions? Commands?
    iii. Are they simple? Compound? Complex? Compound/complex? Minor?
    iv. Are they balanced? Any parallelisms or antithetical structures?
    v. Are there any interesting transitions between sentences?

Textual Analysis of the Narrative 95

3. What are the clauses like?
   i. Other than basic clauses, are there any complement clauses? Are they finite or non-finite? Do they modify verbs or nouns?
   ii. Where is the main finite verb positioned? Early or late in the sentence?
   iii. Are the main clauses fronted by subordinate clauses or adverbials? Are they followed by any?
4. What are the phrases like?
   i. What is the balance between noun phrases and verb phrases?
   ii. Are the noun phrases premodified? Are they postmodified?
   iii. Are the verb phrases made of just verbs? Are there any complements or adjuncts?
5. What is the lexis like?
   i. Is the lexis general or specific? Formal or informal? Descriptive or emotive?
   ii. Are the words polysyllabic/Latinate? Are they monosyllabic/Anglo-Saxon?
   iii. How are lexical categories distributed? Are there any that are more prominent?
   iv. Are there any interesting derivational or inflectional morphological patterns?
   v. Are the nouns abstract or concrete? Are there any proper nouns?
   vi. Are there any lexical sets?
   vii. What is the tense and aspect of the verbs?
   viii. Are the verbs non-transitive? Are they transitive? Are they ditransitive? Are they copular verbs?
   ix. Are there any modal verbs? Are there any semi-modal verbs?
   x. How are pronouns used? What about determiners? Are there any conjunctions? Are there any interjections?

Task C
Work in small groups. Consider the following questions, focussing on the effects of linguistic choices in *Eveline*. You should now be making connections between Tasks A and B above.

1. Look at your annotated text. Can you notice any patterns in the frequency and distribution of textual and grammatical features?
2. Revisit Task A, using the detailed information you gathered from Task B.
   i. What is the setting? What is the time and place? What more can you say based on your analysis above? In other words, what are the effects of such features as verb tenses, adverbials, and complement clauses?
   ii. Who are the main characters? Are there any secondary characters? How are they represented? What are the effects of the way nouns, pronouns and proper names are used? How are they modified? Are there any salient descriptions, e.g. through adjectives or complement clauses?
   iii. What do the characters do? What else happens? How are events and experiences represented? In other words, what are the effects of main and subordi-

nate clauses, or adverbials? What can verb transitivity reveal about the effect of characters on other characters or objects and places? What can verb modality reveal about the truth or likelihood of the events described?
  iv. How could any variations in sentence moods, types or constructions, or lexis, reveal a changing viewpoint? In other words, how does the author/narrator manipulate the audience? What features indicate closer proximity to the characters?
  v. How do you appreciate the text? What aspects of flow or rhythm or imagery do you admire?

Exploring & Writing

Task A

1. Indecision is a common narrative theme. You can explore more narratives about indecision by searching 'stories about indecision'.[1]

    Choose a narrative about indecision which you like. (One suggestion is Ernest Hemingway's *Hills Like White Elephants* (1927) which is also based on a theme of the indecision of a main character.)
2. Work with a partner. Explain your reasons for selecting your narrative.
3. Make brief points for your partner about your chosen narrative under each of the following headings:

   - Setting(s)
   - Main protagonist and other characters
   - Events
   - Narrative voice(s)

4. Use the questions in Task B above to explore how the language of the narrative allows the author to craft some of the foci in 3 above.
5. Compare your chosen narrative to Joyce's *Eveline*. Are there similarities in terms of narrative voice, plot, time layers, characters, setting, objects, imagery etc.?

    Consider the grammatical structures through which your narrative depicts the theme of indecision. Do you see any similarities with Joyce's use of grammatical structures?

---

[1] At the time of printing, the following was available: https://medium.com/the-junction/to-decide-and-to-move-on-79d75328dbe2

Review & Reflection

Task A

In a group, discuss the following:

  i. What might be the most natural way to approach a narrative for the first time?
 ii. What are the first questions you ask yourselves? What do you want to know?
iii. How important to you is the language and style of the narrative?
 iv. How can a grammatical analysis enhance your understanding of the text?
  v. How can a grammatical analysis help you gain insight about the way a narrative is crafted?

Short Narrative 2
A Woman's College from the Outside by Virginia Woolf (1926)

We present our second short narrative, Virginia Woolf's *A Woman's College from the Outside*. The story is centred around Angela, a college student who feels trapped between her parent's desire for upward mobility and independence, the harsh reality of college life, and her awareness of the limits of a patriarchal society.

Chapters 13 and 14 use this narrative to review the materials of Chapters 1, 2, 3, 4, 5, 6, 7, 8, 9, 10, 11 and 12. It is an opportunity to revise the terminology and apply what you have learnt to a new text.

A Woman's College from the Outside

The feathery-white moon never let the sky grow dark; all night the chestnut blossoms were white in the green, and dim was the cow-parsley in the meadows. Neither to Tartary nor to Arabia went the wind of the Cambridge courts, but lapsed dreamily in the midst of grey-blue clouds over the roofs of Newnham. There, in the garden, if she needed space to wander, she might find it among the trees; and as none but women's faces could meet her face, she might unveil it blank, featureless, and gaze into rooms where at that hour, blank, featureless, eyelids white over eyes, ringless hands extended upon sheets, slept innumerable women. But here and there a light still burned.

A double light one might figure in Angela's room, seeing how bright Angela herself was, and how bright came back the reflection of herself from the square glass. The whole of her was perfectly delineated—perhaps the soul. For the glass held up an untrembling image—white and gold, red slippers, pale hair with blue stones in it, and never a ripple or shadow to break the smooth kiss of Angela and her reflection in the glass, as if she were glad to be Angela. Anyhow the moment was glad the bright picture hung in the heart of night, the shrine hollowed in the nocturnal blackness. Strange indeed to have this visible proof of the rightness of things; this lily floating flawless upon Time's pool, fearless, as if this were sufficient—this reflection. Which meditation she betrayed by turning, and the mirror held nothing at all, or only the brass bedstead, and she, running here and there, patting, and darting, became like a woman in a house, and changed again, pursing her lips over a black book and marking with her finger what surely could not be a firm grasp of the science of economics. Only Angela Williams was at Newnham for the purpose of earning her living, and could not forget even in moments of impassioned adoration the cheques of her father at Swansea; her mother washing in the scullery: pink frocks out to dry on the line; tokens that even the lily no longer floats flawless upon the pool, but has a name on a card like another.

A. Williams—one may read it in the moonlight; and next to it some Mary or Eleanor, Mildred, Sarah, Phoebe upon square cards on their doors. All names, nothing but names. The cool white light withered them and starched them until it seemed as if the only purpose of all these names was to rise martially in order should there be a call on them to extinguish a fire, suppress an insurrection, or pass an examination. Such is the power of names written upon cards pinned upon doors. Such too the resemblance, what with tiles, corridors, and bedroom doors, to dairy or nunnery, a place of seclusion or discipline, where the bowl of milk stands cool and pure and there's a great washing of linen.

At that very moment soft laughter came from behind a door. A primvoiced lock struck the hour—one, two. Now if the clock were issuing his commands, they were disregarded. Fire, insurrection, examination, were all snowed under by laughter, or softly uprooted, the sound seeming to bubble up from the depths and gently waft away the hour, rules, discipline. The bed was strewn with cards. Sally was on the floor. Helena in the chair. Good Bertha clasping her hands by the fire-place. A. Williams came in yawning.

'Because it's utterly and intolerably damnable,' said Helena.

'Damnable,' echoed Bertha. Then yawned.

'We're not eunuchs.'

'I saw her slipping in by the back gate with that old hat on. They don't want us to know.'

'They?' said Angela. 'She.'

Then the laughter.

The cards were spread, falling with their red and yellow, faces on the table, and hands were dabbled in the cards. Good Bertha, leaning with her head against the chair, sighed profoundly. For she would willingly have slept, but since night is free pasturage, a limitless field, since night is unmoulded richness, one must tunnel into its darkness. One must hang it with jewels. Night was shared in secret, day browsed on by the whole flock. The blinds were up. A mist was on the garden. Sitting on the floor by the window (while the others played), body, mind, both together, seemed blown through the air, to trail across the bushes. Ah, but she desired to stretch out in bed and to sleep! She believed that no one felt her desire for sleep; she believed humbly—sleepily—with sudden nods and lurchings, that other people were wide awake. When they laughed all together a bird chirped in its sleep out in the garden, as if the laughter...

Yes, as if the laughter (for she dozed now) floated out much like mist and attached itself by soft elastic shreds to plants and bushes, so that the garden was vaporous and clouded. And then, swept by the wind, the bushes would bow themselves and the white vapour blow off across the world.

From all the rooms where women slept this vapour issued, attaching itself to shrubs, like mist, and then blew freely out into the open. Elderly women slept, who would on waking immediately clasp the ivory rod of office. Now smooth and colourless, reposing deeply, they lay surrounded, lay supported, by the bodies of youth recumbent or grouped at the window; pouring forth into the garden this bubbling laughter, this irresponsible laughter: this laughter of mind and body floating away rules, hours, discipline: immensely fertilising, yet formless, chaotic, trailing and straying and tufting the rose-bushes with shreds of vapour.

'Ah,' breathed Angela, standing at the window in her night-gown. Pain was in her voice. She leant her head out. The mist was cleft as if her voice parted it. She had been talking, while the others played, to Alice Avery, about Bamborough Castle; the colour of the sands at evening; upon which Alice said she would write and settle the day, in August, and stooping, kissed her, at least touched her head with her hand, and Angela, positively unable to sit still, like one possessed of a wind-lashed sea in her heart, roamed up and down the room (the witness of such a scene) throwing her arms out to relieve this excitement, this astonishment at the incredible stooping of the miraculous tree with the golden fruit at its summit—hadn't it dropped into her arms? She held it glowing to her breast, a thing not to be touched, thought of, or spoken about, but left to glow there. And then, slowly putting there her stockings, there her slippers, folding her petticoat neatly on top, Angela, her other name being Williams, realised—how could she express it?—that after the dark churning of myriad ages here was light at the end of the tunnel; life; the world. Beneath her it lay—all good; all lovable. Such was her discovery.

Indeed, how could one then feel surprise if, lying in bed, she could not close her eyes?—something irresistibly unclosed them—if in the shallow darkness chair and chest of drawers looked stately, and the looking-glass precious with its ashen hint of day? Sucking her thumb like a child (her age nineteen last November), she lay in this good world, this new world, this world at the end of the tunnel, until a desire to see it or forestall it drove her, tossing her blankets, to guide herself to the window, and there, looking out upon the garden, where the mist lay, all the windows open, one fiery-bluish, something murmuring in the distance, the world of course, and the morning coming, 'Oh,' she cried, as if in pain.

Chapter 13
Moving on 1: A Holistic Review of Chaps. 2, 3, 4, 5, 6, 7, 8, 9 and 10 Based on Narrative 2

In Essence

In this chapter we begin work on our second narrative *A Woman's College from the Outside* by Virginia Woolf (1926). The chapter explores the narrative by considering Woolf's use of the grammatical elements we have considered in previous chapters. We do this in the same order as we considered Joyce's uses, moving from lexical items, through phrases and clauses to sentences and the whole text. This approach ensures your understanding and application of the metalanguage of the grammatical analysis covered in previous chapters whilst also preparing you for a holistic appreciation of the text in Chap. 14. Please note, though, there is no intention to review everything covered in previous chapters: the focus is rather on exploring the salient features of the new text.

As this is a review chapter, we move immediately to analysis of the new text and conclude the chapter by inviting you to reflect on the narrative. We include chapter numbers and headings in brackets after each task so you can, if you wish, easily look back to the chapter in which we first covered a level of analysis.

Textual Analysis

Task A (2 Morphemes, Words and Lexical Categories)
Look at the first sentence of the narrative.

The feathery-white moon never let the sky grow dark; all night the <u>chestnut</u> blossoms were <u>white</u> in the <u>green</u>, and <u>dim</u> was the cow-parsley in the meadows.

1. For each of the underlined words, decide if it functions in the sentence as a noun or as an adjective.

2. How many words function as adjectives in the sentence?
3. Identify the nouns and adjectives depicting colour in the following 10 excerpts (listed in order).

   i. *grey-blue clouds*
   ii. *eyelids white over eyes*
   iii. *For the glass held up an untrembling image—white and gold, red slippers, pale hair with blue stones in it*
   iv. *the nocturnal blackness*
   v. *a black book*
   vi. *pink frocks out to dry*
   vii. *The cool white light*
   viii. *The cards were spread, falling with their red and yellow, faces on the table*
   ix. *the golden fruit at its summit*
   x. *all the windows open, one fiery-bluish*

4. What do you see as the significance of white and black in the narrative? What about other colours?

Task B (2 Morphemes, Words and Lexical Categories)

1. What is similar about the morphology of the following adjectives?

   featureless   flawless   fearless   limitless

2. Comment on the morphology of the following adjectives.

   innumerable   untrembling   unmoulded   irresponsible

3. What effects does Woolf create with use of the adjectives in 1 and 2 above?

Task C (2 Morphemes, Words and Lexical Categories)

1. The narrative contains a lexical set of nouns of place. Here are some examples.

   Outside
   Meadows
   Garden
   Room
   Corridors
   Window

   Identify three more items in the narrative which belong to the same set.

2. Divide the set into two groups. What do you see as the significance of each of the groups?

Task D (3 Nouns and Noun Phrases)

1. The following noun phrases are used to refer to the main protagonist. Number the phrases in the order in which they are first introduced.

   A. *Williams*

> *Angela*
> *Angela, her other name being Williams*
> *She*
> *Angela Williams*

2. What are the effects?
3. Identify the head nouns in the noun phrases in the following excerpts.

   > *this bubbling laughter, this irresponsible laughter: this laughter of mind and body floating away rules, hours, discipline*
   > *this good world, this new world, this world at the end of the tunnel*

4. What is similar about the structures? What effect does the repetition create?
5. *There, in the garden, if she needed space to wander, she might find it among the trees; and as none but women's faces could meet her face, she might unveil it blank, featureless, and gaze into rooms where at that hour, blank, featureless, eyelids white over eyes, ringless hands extended upon sheets, slept innumerable women.*

   What do the pronouns '*it*' in the sentence above refer to?
   How are the nouns '*space*' and '*rooms*' postmodified?
   The adjectives '*blank, featureless*' appear twice in the sentence. What is the structural difference between the two uses?
   How many noun phrases does the sentence contain?
   What are the effects of ending the sentence with a noun phrase?
6. Identify the head nouns and noun phrases in the excerpts below. What is similar about the postmodification of the phrases?

   > *a place of seclusion or discipline, where the bowl of milk stands cool and pure*
   > *From all the rooms where women slept this vapour issued*
   > *Elderly women slept, who would on waking immediately clasp the ivory rod of office*
   > *the garden, where the mist lay*

Task E (4 Verbs 1: Tense and Aspect)

1. What is the tense and aspect of most of the verbs in the narrative?
2. Comment on the tense of the following two pairs of excerpts.

   > *even the lily no longer floats flawless upon the pool, but has a name on a card like another*
   > *Such is the power of names written upon cards pinned upon doors. Such too the resemblance, what with tiles, corridors, and bedroom doors, to dairy or nunnery, a place of seclusion or discipline, where the bowl of milk stands cool and pure and there's a great washing of linen.*
   > *She had been talking, while the others played*
   > *hadn't it dropped into her arms?*

   Why do you think Woolf uses them?
3. Why are the singular nouns followed by 'were' in these examples?

as if she were glad to be Angela
as if this were sufficient
if the clock were issuing his commands

4. What is the mood indicated by most verb forms in the narrative?
5. Why does *'We're not eunuchs.'* Stand out?

Task F (5 Verbs 2: Modality, Catenation, Multi-Word Verbs)

1. Identify the modal verbs in the following twelve excerpts. What are their meanings?

    i. *if she needed space to wander, she might find it among the trees*
    ii. *none but women's faces could meet her face*
    iii. *she might unveil it blank, featureless*
    iv. *A double light one might figure in Angela's room*
    v. *Only Angela Williams was at Newnham for the purpose of earning her living, and could not forget even in moments of impassioned adoration the cheques of her father at Swansea*
    vi. *she would willingly have slept*
    vii. *one must tunnel into its darkness. One must hang it with jewels.*
    viii. *the bushes would bow themselves*
    ix. *Elderly women slept, who would on waking immediately clasp the ivory rod of office.*
    x. *how could she express it?*
    xi. *how could one then feel surprise if, lying in bed, she could not close her eyes?*

2. Do the same modals in the above excerpts always express the same meanings?
3. Suggest why modal verbs are used frequently in the narrative.

Task G (6 Verb Phrases)

1. Identify the seven copular verbs in the excerpts below.

    all night the chestnut blossoms were white in the green
    dim was the cow-parsley in the meadows
    But here and there a light still burned
    The blinds were up.
    A mist was on the garden
    The mist was cleft
    Such was her discovery.
    chair and chest of drawers looked stately

2. Which copular verb links its subject and complement in an unusual order? What are the effects?
3. What effects does the frequent use of copulas have on the narrative?

Textual Analysis

Task H (6 Verb Phrases)

1. In the following phrases, non-finite verbs are used as complements. In each case, identify whether they act as complements of the subject or object.

   A. Williams came in yawning.
   'I saw her slipping in by the back gate with that old hat on…'
   Good Bertha, leaning with her head against the chair, sighed profoundly
   From all the rooms where women slept this vapour issued, attaching itself to shrubs
   'Ah,' breathed Angela, standing at the window in her night-gown
   Angela, positively unable to sit still, like one possessed of a wind lashed sea in her heart, roamed up and down the room (the witness of such a scene) throwing her arms out to relieve this excitement

2. What is unusual about the complementizer in the following example?

   Sitting on the floor by the window (while the others played), body, mind, both together, seemed blown through the air, to trail across the bushes.

3. Identify two further examples in the narrative of non-finite verbs acting as complements.
4. What cumulative effects does Woolf create?

Task I (7 Basic Clauses)

1. Identify the clause structures of the following excerpts.

   A. Williams came in yawning
   Sally was on the floor
   A primvoiced clock struck the hour
   The cool white light withered them
   one may read it
   soft laughter came from behind a door

2. The narrative has few examples of S V O clauses. Why do you think this is?

Task J (8 Sentences)

1. Identify the following sentence types of the excerpts below.

   Simple
   Compound
   Complex
   Compound/complex
   Minor

   a. *At that very moment soft laughter came from behind a door.*

   b. *'Because it's utterly and intolerably damnable,'*

   c. *Then the laughter.*

d. *all night the chestnut blossoms were white in the green, and dim was the cow-parsley in the meadows.*

e. *The mist was cleft as if her voice parted it.*

f. *There, in the garden, if she needed space to wander, she might find it among the trees; and as none but women's faces could meet her face, she might unveil it blank, featureless, and gaze into rooms where at that hour, blank, featureless, eyelids white over eyes, ringless hands extended upon sheets, slept innumerable women.*

2. What type of sentences are the following?

   For the glass held up an untrembling image—white and gold, red slippers, pale hair with blue stones in it, and never a ripple or shadow to break the smooth kiss of Angela and her reflection in the glass, as if she were glad to be Angela.
   Strange indeed to have this visible proof of the rightness of things; this lily floating flawless upon Time's pool, fearless, as if this were sufficient—this reflection.
   Now if the clock were issuing his commands, they were disregarded.
   The mist was cleft as if her voice parted it.
   The cool white light withered them and starched them until it seemed as if the only purpose of all these names was to rise martially in order should there be a call on them to extinguish a fire, suppress an insurrection, or pass an examination.

   How do the dependent clauses attenuate the meanings of their main clauses in the sentences above?

3. Which of the sentence types in 1 above do you think occur most often in the narrative? Why do you think this is? What are the effects?

4. Some of the minor sentences in the narrative are ellipted. What elements are 'missing' from the two examples below?

   Strange indeed to have this visible proof of the rightness of things; this lily floating flawless upon Time's pool, fearless, as if this were sufficient—this reflection.
   Such too the resemblance, what with tiles, corridors, and bedroom doors, to dairy or nunnery, a place of seclusion or discipline, where the bowl of milk stands cool and pure and there's a great washing of linen.

   Why do you think Woolf chooses not to include the ellipted elements?

Task K (9 Clauses Revisited)

1. Identify the adverbials in the following excerpts.

   But here and there a light still burned.
   Anyhow the moment was glad the bright picture hung in the heart of night, the shrine hollowed in the nocturnal blackness.

> *the cheques of her father at Swansea; her mother washing in the scullery: pink frocks out to dry on the line*
> *At that very moment soft laughter came from behind a door.*
> *Night was shared in secret*
> *Beneath her it lay—all good; all lovable*

2. In this narrative, what do most of the adverbials refer to? What are the cumulative effects of the reference of the adverbials?
3. What is unusual about the ordering of clause elements in the following excerpts?

> *Neither to Tartary nor to Arabia went the wind of the Cambridge courts*
> *Only Angela Williams was at Newnham for the purpose of earning her living, and could not forget even in moments of impassioned adoration the cheques of her father at Swansea; her mother washing in the scullery: pink frocks out to dry on the line; tokens that even the lily no longer floats flawless upon the pool, but has a name on a card like another.*
> *She had been talking, while the others played, to Alice Avery, about Bamborough Castle; the colour of the sands at evening; upon which Alice said she would write and settle the day, in August, and stooping, kissed her, at least touched her head with her hand, and Angela, positively unable to sit still, like one possessed of a wind-lashed sea in her heart, roamed up and down the room (the witness of such a scene) throwing her arms out to relieve this excitement, this astonishment at the incredible stooping of the miraculous tree with the golden fruit at its summit—hadn't it dropped into her arms?*

What effects does Woolf create?

Task L (10 Sentences and the Text)

1. The following excerpts contain interrogatives. Who are they asked by, and who to?

> *She had been talking, while the others played, to Alice Avery, about Bamborough Castle; the colour of the sands at evening; upon which Alice said she would write and settle the day, in August, and stooping, kissed her, at least touched her head with her hand, and Angela, positively unable to sit still, like one possessed of a wind-lashed sea in her heart, roamed up and down the room (the witness of such a scene) throwing her arms out to relieve this excitement, this astonishment at the incredible stooping of the miraculous tree with the golden fruit at its summit—hadn't it dropped into her arms?*
> *And then, slowly putting there her stockings, there her slippers, folding her petticoat neatly on top, Angela, her other name being Williams, realised—how could she express it?—that after the dark churning of myriad ages here was light at the end of the tunnel; life; the world.*
> *Indeed, how could one then feel surprise if, lying in bed, she could not close her eyes?—something irresistibly unclosed them—if in the shallow darkness chair and chest of drawers looked stately, and the looking-glass precious with its ashen hint of day?*

2. What is similar about the structures of the underlined clauses in the sentences below?

> Now if the clock were issuing his commands, <u>they were disregarded</u>.
> The cards were spread, falling with their red and yellow, faces on the table, and <u>hands were dabbled in the cards.</u>
> <u>Night was shared in secret</u>, <u>day browsed on</u> by the whole flock.
> Sitting on the floor by the window (while the others played), <u>body, mind, both together, seemed blown through the air</u>, to trail across the bushes.
> She held it glowing to her breast, <u>a thing not to be touched, thought of, or spoken about, but left to glow</u> there

3. What effects does the use of the construction create?
4. What unusual feature do the constructions of the following sentences share?

> *For the glass held up an untrembling image—white and gold, red slippers, pale hair with blue stones in it, and never a ripple or shadow to break the smooth kiss of Angela and her reflection in the glass, as if she were glad to be Angela.*
> *Which meditation she betrayed by turning, and the mirror held nothing at all, or only the brass bedstead, and she, running here and there, patting, and darting, became like a woman in a house, and changed again, pursing her lips over a black book and marking with her finger what surely could not be a firm grasp of the science of economics.*
> *For she would willingly have slept, but since night is free pasturage, a limitless field, since night is unmoulded richness, one must tunnel into its darkness. Such was her discovery.*

What effect does this create?

Task M (10 Sentences and the Text)

1. The narrative includes the following discourse markers.

    Anyhow   Strange   indeed   Only   Indeed   Yes

    Whose voice do they represent?
    Who narrates the narrative?

2. The narrative has seven instances of the use of direct speech, but no reported speech. What effects does this have?
3. Woolf punctuates several of the sentences using dashes (–).

    The whole of her was perfectly delineated—perhaps the soul. For the glass held up an untrembling image—white and gold, red slippers, pale hair with blue stones in it, and never a ripple or shadow to break the smooth kiss of Angela and her reflection in the glass, as if she were glad to be Angela.

    What effects are created?
    Look at other instances of the use of dashes later in the narrative. Are the effects similar?

4. Comment on the use of parallelisms in the following excerpts.

   There, in the garden, if she needed space to wander, she might find it among the trees; and as none but women's faces could meet her face, she might unveil it blank, featureless, and gaze into rooms where at that hour, blank, featureless, eyelids white over eyes, ringless hands extended upon sheets, slept innumerable women.

   Now smooth and colourless, reposing deeply, they lay surrounded, lay supported, by the bodies of youth recumbent or grouped at the window; pouring forth into the garden this bubbling laughter, this irresponsible laughter: this laughter of mind and body floating away rules, hours, discipline: immensely fertilising, yet formless, chaotic, trailing and straying and tufting the rose-bushes with shreds of vapour.

   Find another example of a parallelism in the narrative.
   What cumulative effects do the parallelisms create?
5. The narrative contains a lexical set of white objects. Identify three items which belong to this set.
   What images are created?
   Comment on the use of references to brightness and reflections throughout the narrative.

Review & Reflection

Task A
Which features explored above do you consider most significant to the way Woolf's narrative 'works'?

Task B
At points, the narrative blurs a boundary between prose and poetry. Do you agree? Why/why not?

Chapter 14
Moving on 2: A Holistic Appreciation of Narrative 2

In Essence

This final review chapter based on *A Woman's College from the Outside* by Virginia Woolf (1926) adopts a whole text approach to appreciate connections between the narrative and its language, thus coming closer to a stylistic analysis of the text. We end this chapter by suggesting an overall approach to analysing grammar in literature which you can then apply to any text of your choice. We also come full circle by revisiting some of the questions about the roles of grammar in writing which we posed in Chap. 1.

Check the Basics

Similar to Chap. 12, in this chapter we invite you to apply your knowledge and insight of grammar in a holistic way to the text. We take again a top-down approach to analysis, beginning with general aspects of the narrative and the text, and proceeding to more particular aspects of sentences, clauses, phrases and lexical items—again, working backwards from Chapter 10 to 2. As we suggested previously, this allows us to enhance our understanding of grammar in a more holistic way, so that our initial questions about the narrative and its aims are revisited following a grammatical analysis.

The tasks under Textual Analysis are the same as in Chap. 12 and are reprinted here for convenience. In Exploring & Writing, we formulate a template that you can use to analyse any narrative. The steps we follow are the same:

- Approaching the narrative: initial questions
- Analysing the text: grammar and lexis
- Interpreting the text: meaning and effects

Textual Analysis of the Narrative

Task A
Work in small groups. Looking at *A Woman's College from the Outside,* consider the following questions focussing on general aspects of narrative and the text.

1. What is this narrative about?

    i. What is the setting? What is the time and place?
    ii. Who are the main characters? Are there any secondary characters?
    iii. What do the characters do? What else happens?

2. Who is the narrative told by?

    i. Whose voice do you hear?
    ii. Are there any other voices represented?
    iii. Whose point of view is represented?

3. How is the narrative structured?

    i. Is the narrative chronological and linear?
    ii. Are there any points where the narrative structure and actual order of events differ from each other?

Task B
Work in small groups. Looking at *A Woman's College from the Outside,* consider the following questions focussing on the text and its grammatical structures and lexis. You may want to annotate the text, or use highlighting, colour-coding, circling or underlining. These visual cues will help you assess the frequency and distribution of textual and grammatical features. As you consider each level of analysis below, look particularly for patterns and features which are common or repeated as well as for features which stand out because of their contrast or difference or absence.

1. How is the text structured?

    i. How many paragraphs are there?
    ii. How long are the paragraphs?
    iii. What is the transition between paragraphs?
    iv. Are there any interesting openers? Are there any noticeable expansion patterns, in other words, how do the paragraphs develop?
    v. Are there any interesting punctuation patterns?

2. What are the sentences like?

    i. Are they long or short?
    ii. Are they statements? Questions? Commands?
    iii. Are they simple? Compound? Complex? Compound/complex? Minor?
    iv. Are they balanced? Any parallelisms or antithetical structures?
    v. Are there any interesting transitions between sentences?

3. What are the clauses like?

    i. Other than basic clauses, are there any complement clauses? Are they finite or non-finite? Do they modify verbs or nouns?
    ii. Where is the main finite verb positioned? Early or late in the sentence?
    iii. Are the main clauses fronted by subordinate clauses or adverbials? Are they followed by any?

4. What are the phrases like?

    i. What is the balance between noun phrases and verb phrases?
    ii. Are the noun phrases premodified? Are they postmodified?
    iii. Are the verb phrases made of just verbs? Are there any complements or adjuncts?

5. What is the lexis like?

    i. Is the lexis general or specific? Formal or informal? Descriptive or emotive?
    ii. Are the words polysyllabic/ Latinate? Are they monosyllabic/ Anglo-Saxon?
    iii. How are lexical categories distributed? Are there any that are more prominent?
    iv. Are there any interesting derivational or inflectional morphological patterns?
    v. Are the nouns abstract or concrete? Are there any proper nouns?
    vi. Are there any lexical sets?
    vii. What is the tense and aspect of the verbs?
    viii. Are the verbs non-transitive? Are they transitive? Are they ditransitive? Are they copular verbs?
    ix. Are there any modal verbs? Are there any semi-modals?
    x. How are pronouns used? What about determiners? Are there any conjunctions? Are there any interjections?

Task C

Work in small groups. Consider the following questions, focussing on the effects of linguistic choices in *A Woman's College from the Outside*. You should now be making connections between Tasks A and B above.

1. Look at your annotated text. Can you notice any patterns in the frequency and distribution of textual and grammatical features?
2. Revisit Task A, using the detailed information you gathered from Task B.

    i. What is the setting? What is the time and place? What more can you say based on your analysis above? In other words, what are the effects of such features as verb tenses, adverbials, and complement clauses?
    ii. Who are the main characters? Are there any secondary characters? How are they represented? What are the effects of the way nouns, pronouns and proper names are used? How are they modified? Are there any salient descriptions, e.g. through adjectives or complement clauses?

iii. What do the characters do? What else happens? How are events and experiences represented? In other words, what are the effects of main and subordinate clauses, or adverbials? What can verb transitivity reveal about the effect of characters on other characters or objects and places? What can verb modality reveal about the truth or likelihood of the events described?
iv. How could any variations in sentence moods, types or constructions, or lexis, reveal a changing viewpoint? In other words, how does the author/narrator manipulate the audience? What features indicate closer proximity to the characters?
v. How do you appreciate the text? What aspects of flow or rhythm or imagery do you admire?

Exploring & Writing

Task A
Below is a more diagrammatic way to represent a summary of the analysis questions in the tasks above.

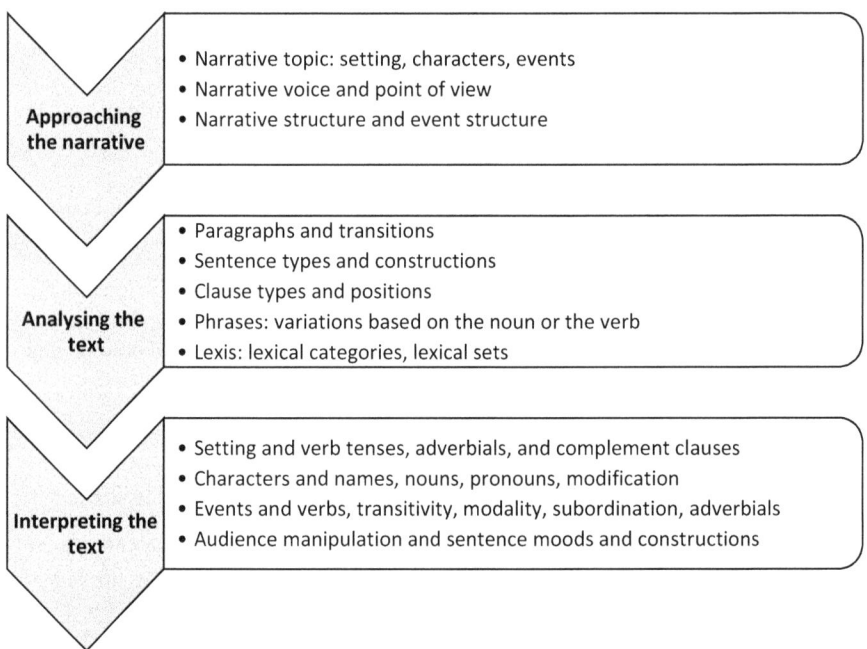

You can use the diagram (or the more detailed questions above) to analyse a narrative you like, or one you have written.

Task B
1. Take a narrative you have written yourself and revisit your lexical and grammatical choices. Can you think of alternative choices drawing on the questions above?
2. How do you think pursuing a grammatical analysis like this could enhance your prose?

A Note on Textual Analysis

To appreciate any text, you need to do much more than play 'I-spy' with its features. Essentially, you need to consider the impacts of the uses of grammatical features, (including cumulative impacts and how features interrelate, interact and contrast). You need to be aware, of course, that readers can appreciate a text without consciously reflecting on the language which 'delivers' it. You also need to be aware that that any text impacts differently on different readers (and even on the same reader at different times).

As you will certainly realize by now, consideration of the role of grammar (and related features in a text) is never scientific and is always subject to the personal 'lens' through which individual readers view, interpret and appreciate the text.

What we include in this book is a preliminary attempt at stylistic analysis which focuses on grammatical aspects only. Grammar is of course one of the concerns of stylisticians, along with many other textual features such as metaphor, imagery and rhetorical devices. The further reading section includes a few recommendations of Stylistics textbooks for those who are interested.

Review & Reflection

Task A
We began, in Chap. 1, by considering Joan Didion's analogies that liken an author working with grammar to a musician playing a piano and a photographer taking a picture.

> *Grammar is a piano I play by ear, since I seem to have been out of school the year the rules were mentioned. All I know about grammar is its infinite power. To shift the structure of a sentence alters the meaning of that sentence, as definitely and inflexibly as the position of a camera alters the meaning of the object photographed. Many people know about camera angles now, but not so many know about sentences. The arrangement of the words matters, and the arrangement you want can be found in the picture in your mind. The picture dictates the arrangement. The picture dictates whether this will be a sentence with or without clauses, a sentence that ends hard or a dying-fall sentence, long or short, active or passive. The picture tells you how to arrange the words and the arrangement of the words tells you, or tells me, what's going on in the picture. Nota bene.*
>   *It tells you.*
>   *You don't tell it.*

1. Discuss these analogies. How far do they work for you? Which do you prefer?
2. Suggest your own analogy for the use of grammar in creative writing. Compare your ideas with your group. Which analogies do you like best?

Task B
1. Discuss what you personally have learnt about grammar and about grammar in literature from working through the chapters on Joyce's and Woolf's narratives.
2. Which information and activities have been most useful to you? Why?

Task C
1. Do you agree conscious awareness of grammatical possibilities is a feature of good writing? Discuss your thoughts with your group.
2. What about good reading?
3. How do you think your knowledge and insight can support your own future studies and/or literary creations?
4. Discuss your thoughts about Task C with your group. Add any other thoughts or questions which working through this book has raised for you.

Suggested Answers

Our 'answers' in the following sections are mainly offered as broad recommendations rather than as definitive or comprehensive statements. This is particularly true of our answers to the Exploring and Writing sections. We provide suggested 'answers' to all our tasks in all chapters, even the most exploratory and creative. Obviously, many of these tasks do not have 'answers' in the sense of being right or wrong, but we hope you will find it useful to compare your own suggestions with ours. You will find that our answers to open-ended questions, especially, aim to show you a direction of thinking and to encourage you to explore further. You will, of course, get most out of the answers by completing the tasks first! We also hope that your group discussions may, at times, generate more ideas and thus produce fuller responses than those suggested in this section. Finally, many of our tasks require not only identification of grammatical features, but also interpretation of their impacts within our selected narratives. Here, we work at an interface between grammar and stylistics. Again, there are no rights or wrongs, we simply offer you our thoughts. It is possible, and even desirable, that your own interpretations may, at times, differ from and go beyond our own.

Chapter 1

Grammar in English

Textual Analysis

Texts A, B and C all emphasize the importance of grammar in writing. Joan Didion talks very eloquently about 'the piano [she] play[s] by ear', an instinctive and unconscious process of creating music driven by the rhythm, the melody, the effect on the ear. It's no coincidence that texts also have 'rhythm'; some texts sound 'good', some less so, some are capable of carrying you away, not unlike your favourite song. ProWritingAid.com advises aspiring writers to 'tap into the logic of rhythm and structure', while Francine Prose also advocates learning 'by positive model'.

Joan Didion uses another metaphor, that of the 'camera', and the more deliberate attempt at arranging the objects and positioning the lens accordingly. Grammar is nothing but an arrangement of words, phrases and sentences which concerns all writers. Many (including Didion) won't have the metalanguage to talk about it, but all will experiment with word order and sentence length to achieve the right meaning and their desired effects.

Exploring & Writing

Task A

This question is a chance to discuss perceptions of the word 'grammar'. It's worth repeating here that grammar is an inherent characteristic of language and refers to the system by which language is organised. Phrases, clauses and sentences are what the English grammatical system is based on. Once we start talking about English structure we refer, of course, to the grammar of English. So all languages have grammars, and are therefore systematic, and each individual grammar applies to each language. In linguistics, grammar comprises morphology and syntax, the study of word and sentence structures respectively. Grammatical theory examines different models, or approaches to understanding grammar, such as Generative Grammar or Systemic Functional Grammar.

Task B

The units of grammatical analysis, from smallest to largest are: (1) morpheme, (2) word, (3) phrase, (4) clause, (5) sentence, (6) paragraph, (7) text. (It is worth noting that some words consist of a single morpheme, some sentences of a single clause, and some texts of a single sentence.)

Task C

Who better than Dickens to illustrate the comment given in question 1! The selected paragraphs are fine examples to illustrate that words alone don't make literature; but what they are as well as how they combine does!

The opening of *A Tale of Two Cities* introduces the theme of duality which is central to the novel. What's good for some is bad for others, and at any one time, the world is full of contradiction. The language supports the topic perfectly. This is achieved, firstly, by the pairing of contrasting concepts: the best of times and the worst of times, wisdom and foolishness, belief and incredulity, light and darkness, hope and despair, having everything and having nothing, Heaven and hell, good and evil. Secondly, the use of parallel structures, repeated phrases at the beginning of each clause, adds both emphasis and rhythm: it was…, it was… (five pairs), we had…, we had… (one pair), we were…, we were… (one pair). This is a fine example where word meaning and sentence structure combine to a powerful effect. What makes this passage so eloquent, evocative and inviting is the juxtaposition of antonyms, words whose meanings cancel each other, and also the simple, steady, predictable, repetitive structure. We don't know whether the word meanings determined the grammar or whether the desire to use short, powerful clauses was Dickens's point of departure, but we do know this is one of the best-crafted, most-loved passages in English.

The second paragraph of *Bleak House* also develops the theme of 'bleak' introduced by the title. Fog has descended on the landscape and it's so overwhelming that it can be seen and heard in every place and by everybody. It's above the city and the countryside, and both the old and the young are affected by it. The passage begins with a short, elliptical sentence: 'Fog everywhere.' Strictly speaking this isn't a grammatical clause in English: you'll learn in later chapters that to have a sentence you need a clause, and to have a clause you need a verb! But you can barely accuse Charles Dickens of breaking the rules of grammar! In later sentences, the author unpacks what he means by "everywhere", mentioning different locations (the meadows, the river, the city, the marshlands of Essex, the hills of Kent, the shipyards and the ships) and different kinds of people (the pensioners, the skipper in his cabin, the young apprentice on the deck, the people on the bridges). The passage is also full of rhythm, each sentence beginning with 'fog' and proceeding with a rather detailed description of places and people. It's a beautiful passage, but also one that displays many of the things that traditional grammar books and style guides tell you to avoid, such as ellipsis and repetition of words and phrases. But it's still one of the most admired passages in the English literary cannon for its ability to portray the intended meaning and generate for the reader a strong feeling, perhaps one of despair, but also one of keen anticipation to keep reading, to find out why all seems so desperately bleak.

Task D

Here's what we came up with, in an attempt to imitate Dickens, touching upon all three suggested themes (home, love, age, young and old):

> *Maplewick bent his aging body into the wind as he made his way homewards across the darkening heath. He drew the orphan boy closer into his chest at every step, while the rain stabbed at his sodden hat with angry fingers. 'Home!' Maplewick cried back to the wind, and again 'home!' To be there with Mrs M, the fire, and a blanket for the infant; and he quickened his step as if dancing with the rain.*

We have tried to include some of the characteristics we came across in Dickens's novels: sentimentality, personification (in this case of the wind and the rain), contrast (the old man and the infant, heat and cold, light and dark), subject matter (orphans, homes), details about the characters, but also the weather and the landscape. Long sentences are another characteristic.

We hope you have begun to understand how difficult it is to write elegant or powerful prose, let alone prose that mimics the style of a great writer! You may have found that working together has helped the process, for example by 'brainstorming' words that describe love or youth or home. Drafting and editing are essential parts of writing, and you may have found that once one of you has come up with a few lines, it's easier for the other person to improve on it. Having said this, everybody has their own style, and it can be tricky to 'share' your voice with another person. In any case, we hope you have become more conscious about the themes we have covered in the chapter, such as the combination of words and structure to convey meaning, or your perception of what might be considered grammatical, acceptable or unacceptable, effective, and so on.

Review & Reflection

Task A

Having finished this chapter, you should be able to answer the question 'What is Grammar?'. You should also be able to explain the role of grammatical as well as lexical choice in effective writing and feel encouraged to proceed with the book and learn grammar from (but also for) literature.

Task B

Didion's observation captures the interdependence between sentence structure and meaning. Take just three words and follow Didion in imagining them as the objects to be photographed. The objects are: *boy, girl, kiss.*

And here are the possible arrangements: (a) The boy kissed the girl. (b) The girl kissed the boy. (c) The girl was kissed by a boy. (d) That girl, a boy kissed her! (e) Kissing, a boy and a girl!

This is an easy example, which shows you how three simple words can be combined in five or more ways, each time meaning something slightly different.

Chapter 2

Morphemes, Words and Lexical Categories

Textual Analysis of the Narrative

Task A

1. Out of context, and if you looked them up in a dictionary, the words in the table are all nouns. However, in the text, some of the nouns perform a different function, i.e. to modify the main noun that follows them. These are: *concrete, cinder, brick, blackthorn*. The nouns in the paragraph are all concrete nouns, and they refer to the people and objects Eveline can either see out of the window or retrieve from her memory of what used to be or happen at that location when she was a child.
2. The majority of the nouns are concrete, as would be expected from the content of the paragraph: Eveline is describing what she sees out of the window, which in turn creates another picture, that of her childhood memory. It is interesting to note how objects are interspersed by people.
3. *People, footsteps, houses, children, roofs, Devines, Waters, Dunns, brothers, sisters* are plural.
4. Joyce uses proper nouns to refer to places, *Belfast, England*, or people, *Devines, Waters, Dunns, Ernest, Keogh, Dizzie Dunn*. We could assume that Ernest held a special place in Eveline's heart as she refers to him by his first name, rather than the vaguer *brother* or *sister*. *Keogh* might have been important to her too (or simply the child was affectionately known *as little Keogh the cripple*), and *Tizzie Dunn*, whose name is given in full perhaps out of respect for the dead. There is a sense in which Eveline echoes the names which have been placed in her head by others. They seem to provide her world with fixed points of reference.
5. Other proper nouns include Miss Gavan and Miss Hill, in reference to the Stores: this is the only mention of Eveline's family name (Hill), in the context of her workplace, a place where the use of surnames may suggest other formality or distance. Eveline's lover is referred to simply as Frank, a sign of familiarity and affection. Poppens is how Frank nicknamed Eveline, again a sign of intimacy. Names of places are also mentioned, in relation to Frank: Canada, Patagonia, Buenos Ayres. In the narrative, it is the choice of proper nouns that's quite revealing, signalling how the protagonist relates to those around her. Overall, it's intriguing to see what Eveline's relationships with others and her attitudes towards them show about her own character. We will return to this theme in our exploration of other grammatical features.

Task B

1. The adjective + noun combinations are: *last house, new red houses, little brown houses, bright houses, shining roofs, little Keogh.*
2. Adjectives can be attributive or predicative. In *little brown houses, bright brick houses, shining roofs* the adjective(s) precede the nouns they describe (attributive position). In her *father was not so bad* and *her mother was alive* the adjective follows a form of the verb *to be* (predicative position) *and* describes what the noun was like at a particular point in time. We learn subsequently that Eveline's father wasn't always 'not so bad', and that her mother had subsequently died. The adjectives are always applied from the perspective of the main character, Eveline. Most of the adjectives in the paragraph are used in the predicative position, indicating permanent characteristics of the objects and people that occupy Eveline's memory.

Task C

1. The missing verbs are *were, was, was, was, were, was, was, had gone, changes, going to go away, to leave.*
2. Without its verbs, the text becomes entirely static. There is little clue as to how the people and objects relate to and act upon each other. Verbs are also marked for tense and are the main indication of time in the story. Without them, the sequence of events in the narrative becomes unclear for the reader.
3. In terms of form, *to go away* is a multi-word verb, *to leave* is a single-word verb. In terms of meaning, the more colloquial going away perhaps suggests longer distance and duration while leaving may not be as permanent.
4. Other examples of multi-word verbs in the narrative include: *draw back* (withdraw), *found out* (discovered) and *running out* (finishing). They are all formed of a main verb combined with a preposition or adverb to produce a composite meaning. As with 'going away' they also all share a more colloquial feeling than their single-word near synonyms. We explore multi-word verbs further in Chap. 5.

    You may also have noticed verb tenses and aspects such as had gone or was going to go. These are not strictly multi-word verbs. We explore verb tenses and aspects further in Chap. 4.
5. *stood, held, knew, speaking* and *saying* are verbs. (*Speaking* and *saying* combine with the auxiliary verb *was* to form a verb aspect. We will say more about this in Chap. 4.)

    Swaying has the form of a verb, but functions here as an adjective to describe the noun *crowd*. English often uses 'ing' verb forms as adjectives e.g. an interesting book.

Suggested Answers

Task D

1. Time is significant in the story as events in the present and in the past, in perception and memory, or indeed the imagining of the future, need to be distinguished.
2. There are many other adverbs in the story: manner (lively, unspeakably, quickly, tightly, awfully, pleasantly, secretly, constantly), frequency (often, usually, regularly), degree (especially, only, nearly, fairly, wholly), time (afterwards, before, latterly, lately).
3. At least a quarter of the words in the paragraph are nouns. The noun to verb ratio is 2:1; the adjective to noun ratio is 1:3; the adverb to verb ratio is 3:4.
4. Content words are significant as they answer the who, what, where, when and how of the story. Nouns in particular are key, as they represent the themes of the story. The introduction of a new noun may change the theme (e.g. look at the first use of the word 'field' in the second paragraph, and how that signals the beginning of a mini sub-narrative of the character's childhood). Detailed descriptions are expressed through a high density of nouns and adjectives, and we find these at moments of intensity, either internal or external. Check out the detail around the 'photograph' in the third paragraph, and Eveline's train of thought as her eyes linger on it. Similarly, in the frantic yet contemplative scene we get to picture the station, the shed, the soldiers, the boat in much detail, as if Eveline's hyperactive brain is noticing everything. Perhaps more surprising is the high frequency of adverbs, which is sometimes also motivated by the content (her contrasted relationship with her father, and Frank, for example, where what happened is scrutinised in detail). Or we could perhaps suggest that they are part of Joyce's authorial style.

Task E

1. The words *go, gone and going* occur frequently, alluding to the themes of departure and migration that underpin the story.
2. *Begin/begun* are repeated regularly as Eveline seeks new beginnings
3. The adjective *unaccustomed* is made up of *custom (free morpheme),* the affix (preceding bound morpheme) *un-* and the suffix (following bound morpheme) *-ed.* The use of such a word is self-referential, that is it draws attention to itself because of its morphological complexity. In a sense, therefore, the form of the word is on this occasion symbolic of its meaning.
4. The *adjectives invariable, unspeakably and undesirable* are also formed of three morphemes and, as in 3 above, *un-* or *in-* negate the meaning of the word they derive from.

Exploring & Writing

Task A

Nouns: *air, atmosphere, cloud, hurricane, sky, storm, tornado, wind*
Verbs: *anticipate, imagine, darken, feel, howl, melt, prove, spin*
Adjectives: *dark, freak, natural, quiet, silent*
Adverbs: *away, independently, now/later, suddenly, here/there*

Here's the beginning of our story, describing an incident:

> *No-one in the village could have anticipated or imagined such an incident. As the sky darkened and the wind began to howl, they at first thought it was some freak storm: a hurricane or a tornado or something new, beyond the categories established by meteorologists. Something new it proved, but this was not natural. At midnight the wind suddenly quietened, and the dark clouds melted away and there, poised above the village of Middlerange, was the silently spinning sphere, as wide as the village itself. Observers later came up independently with the same word for what they felt in the air that night, describing the atmosphere as one of evil.*

Note how some words made their way to the finished text in a modified form, changing their lexical category: quiet (adjective) > quietened (verb); away (adverb) > melted away (multi-word verb); spin (verb) > spinning (adjective). We have also added a noun (sphere), for a sense of mystery, and a fictional village. Feel free to continue the story!

Task B

We have selected three stories we like which were written around the same time as our selected narratives. All are widely available.

Catherine Mansfield's *The daughters of the Late Colonel* (1920) begins with a very short paragraph setting the time, 'the week after' [Colonel's death] and follows with a dialogue between the two daughters, who argue whether they should give their father's top hat to the porter. Given that most of the words would be direct speech, the sentences are bound to be short, and the content would be carried mostly by nouns and verbs; adjectives and adverbs would be low in number.

Elizabeth Bowen's *The Demon Lover* (1945) begins with the main character, Kathleen Drover, returning to her shut-up (due to the blitz) home in London. It's quite an atmospheric part of the story, the streets eerie, the air wet, the house deteriorated. The descriptions are expressed by a combination of nouns and adjectives; verbs are few, because not much is happening.

Ernest Hemingway's *Hills Like White Elephants* (1927) is remarkable for its simplicity of prose and powerful symbolism. The setting drives the story, and the opening lines are significant. We need to pay attention to the hills, the American man, the girl, the express train to Barcelona. Typical of Hemingway, every word here counts, and it wouldn't be too surprising that nouns would be the predominant category.

Suggested Answers   127

Task C

1. This is the beginning of our short story, with nouns deleted:

    With eminent _____ as _____, _____ and _____ had high _____ when the _____ was announced. By _____, in line with _____, they had given away their _____ and _____ and most of their _____. The _____ had been sold and emptied and their _____ had dealt with the electricity _____; the gas _____; local _____; the _____ (to good _____); _____; and all_____. On the last _____ someone collected their _____ at 11.00 and at 12.00 a _____ arrived and took them across open _____ to the_____. By 1.00 they had passed through _____ and climbed up through the _____ into the _____ of the lunar _____.

2. Same, with nouns inserted:

    With eminent <u>scientists</u> as <u>parents</u>, <u>Sally</u> and <u>Glenn</u> had high <u>expectations</u> when The <u>Adventure</u> was announced. By <u>June</u>, in line with <u>instructions</u>, they had given away their <u>toys</u> and <u>books</u> and most of their <u>clothes</u>. The <u>house</u> had been sold and emptied and their <u>parents</u> had dealt with the electricity <u>supply</u>; the gas <u>supply</u>; local <u>taxes</u>; the <u>pets</u> (to good <u>homes</u>); <u>goodbyes</u>; and all <u>lists</u>. On the last <u>day</u> someone collected their <u>car</u> at 11.00 and at 12.00 a <u>bus</u> arrived and took them across open <u>country</u> to the <u>base</u>. By 1.00 they had passed through <u>security</u> and climbed up through the <u>gantry</u> into the <u>nose</u> of the lunar <u>rocket</u>.

3. Discussion:

    Inserting the missing nouns demonstrated the importance of immediate context: some nouns were easy to guess from the words directly before or after (*expectations, instructions, house, supply, taxes, homes, day, car, bus, country*); some would be easy if the lexical field is familiar (*gantry, nose, rocket*); some options were entirely open-ended (*scientists, parents, Adventure, toys, books, clothes, pets, goodbyes, lists, base, security*). The proper names (*Sally, Glenn, June*) would of course be impossible to guess, but their slots should be a little more obvious.

Task D

1. Adding verbs to the above paragraph:

    Verbs are the essence of what actually happened, and you can't add them to an existing narrative without altering the events. You might want to say things like *they had given away their toys, and <u>sold</u> their books and <u>donated</u> most of their clothes*, but this isn't how the author intended it.

2. Adding adjectives and adverbs to the above paragraph:

    Adjectives and adverbs can be added without altering the story, but simply adding more detail to it: *By <u>early (adj.)</u> June, in line with <u>detailed (adj.)</u> instructions, they had given away <u>reluctantly (adv.)</u> their <u>expensive (adj.)</u> toys and precious <u>(adj.)</u> books and most of their <u>beautiful (adj.)</u> clothes.*

3. Effects of additions:

    Adding verbs would introduce new events to the story, just as adding nouns would introduce new themes. Adjectives and adverbs, on the other hand, simply modify the existing nouns and verbs respectively, therefore adding detail. The effect may or may not be desirable, e.g. *the expensive toys precious books and beautiful clothes* which are *reluctantly given away,* add information not there in the original version, but suggesting something about the characters and their actions. That the pets went to *good homes* suffices as a phrase; *good, warm, welcoming homes* feels unnecessarily elaborate.

Review & Reflection

Task A

1. A free morpheme is a word in itself. A bound morpheme is added to a free one for grammatical reasons, or to derive new words.
2. Functions of lexical categories:

> Nouns: names for people, places, things & states e.g. man
> Verbs: words which state actions, events and states e.g. look
> Adjectives: words which describe nouns e.g. dusty
> Adverbs: words which describe verbs e.g. usually
> Determiners: Words which come before nouns to specify which noun e.g. the
> Prepositions: words which describe how something relates to a noun e.g. at
> Pronouns: words which can take the place of nouns e.g. she
> Conjunctions: words which join phrases, clauses and sentences e.g. then

Task B

But in her new home, in a distant unknown country, it would not be like that.

Nouns: *home, country*
Verbs: *would (not) be*
Adjectives: *new, distant, unknown*
Adverbs: *like that* (as a phrase)
Pronouns: *it, that*
Determiners: *her, a*
Prepositions: *in, like*
Conjunctions: *but*
Participles: *not*

Nouns, verbs, adjectives and adverbs are open categories. The rest are closed categories.

Task C

Legal documents usually have a high frequency of nouns followed by verbs.
The bottle of shampoo would describe its contents in several positive words, so the distribution of adjectives would be much higher than in an average text.
The football match would be reported in detail, so expect lots of adverbs of time, place and manner, but also nouns and action verbs.

Suggested Answers

Chapter 3

Nouns and Noun Phrases

Textual Analysis of the Narrative

Task A

1. The head nouns are underlined below:

   the <u>odour</u> of dusty cretonne
   the <u>man</u> out of the last house
   a <u>man</u> from Belfast
   the <u>children</u> of the avenue
   the <u>name</u> of the priest

2. Each head noun is postmodified by a prepositional phrase (preposition + noun phrase), which adds a particular detail about the head noun.

Task B

1. All of the noun phrases given are premodified. The premodification is in the form of a determiner (in the first four examples), followed by a describing or specifying noun or adjective(s).
2. Stylistically, the phrases are of similar weight, which gives rhythm and pace to the piece. Thematically, they reveal detail about what the protagonist sees out of the window or retrieves from memory. This in turn adds imagery (we notice the contrast, for example, between the old little brown houses and the new bright red brick houses) and tells us something about what Eveline considers significant detail, thus aiding her characterisation.

Task C

1. The head nouns are underlined below:

   its familiar <u>objects</u> which she had dusted once a week for so many years
   those familiar <u>objects</u> from which she had never dreamed of being divided
   the <u>name</u> of the priest whose yellowing photograph hung on the wall above the broken harmonium beside the coloured print of the promises made to Blessed Margaret Mary Alacoque

The first two are similar in structure, again creating rhythm in the narrative. The third is much more elaborate, as if Eveline's stare lingers for longer; the faster or more intense the train of thought the longer and more complex the structure, a feature typical of stream-of-consciousness writing.

2. The head nouns are underlined below:

> <u>He</u> would save <u>her</u>

The two noun phrases here (subject and object) consist of a single pronoun, with no pre- or postmodification. The sentence is short, sharp, powerful, in line with its content, what Eveline hopes or expects will happen.

Task D

1. Joyce uses the phrase 'the odour of dusty cretonne' twice, as follows:

> *Her head was leaned against the window curtains and in her nostrils was <u>the odour of dusty cretonne.</u>*
> *Her time was running out but she continued to sit by the window, leaning her head against the window curtain, inhaling <u>the odour of dusty cretonne.</u>*

The meaning is significant. One might argue that dust doesn't smell, yet we may also assume it did in Eveline's room. The phrase is of course symbolic of time passed, the image is of a modest, dusty, smelly old room which suffocates the young girl; this is in contrast to the world outside where she could be free, the new country that awaits her, full of the hope of youth. The repetition of the phrase (the only repeated phrase in the narrative) seems to indicate her inability to escape her surroundings, as she breathes them in, so they become part of her.

2. Eveline is seen by the window on two occasions:

> *She sat at the window watching the evening invade the avenue. Her head was leaned against the window curtains and in her nostrils was the odour of dusty cretonne.*
> *Her time was running out but she continued to sit by the window, leaning her head against the window curtain, inhaling the odour of dusty cretonne.*

A considerable time must have elapsed between the two occurrences, indicated by their position in the text, and reinforced by lexical means, such as the 'evening invading', then 'deepening' as the room was getting darker. On both occasions we see 'her head' leaning against 'the window curtain'. 'Her head' is significant: Was she tired? Worried? Troubled? The 'window curtains' are also a key motif; the same curtains that shut the view of the world outside, that trap her indoors, the old, smelly, heavy cloth that stifles her. In short, time has passed, but little has changed for Eveline.

3. We find 'black' on two occasions:

> *her black leather purse*
> *the black mass of the boat*

In both cases 'black' is an attributive adjective, describing the colour of the leather purse and the boat respectively. We might want to guess that the second meaning is more than just a reference to the colour of the ship, alluding something that's not only vast but also sinister.

Suggested Answers 131

4. Joyce uses several premodified noun phrases with negative connotations:

    yellowing photograph, broken harmonium, hard work, hard life, undesirable life, ghost stories, dark room, melancholy air, pitiful vision, mournful whistle, helpless animal

These are distributed throughout the story, emphasising the adversity of the main character in both her past and present, and, overall, lending the story an air of gloomy pessimism.

5. The noun phrases *a hard life, a wholly undesirable life, another life* all have premodified noun phrases with *life* as their head noun. The first two refer to the past and present situation, which is unpleasant; 'another life' refers to the future. The similarity of the structures strongly suggests the future life may be similar to that of the past and present.

Task E

1. The noun phrases all contain postmodification of the head nouns (*seas, cry* and *sign*) by a prepositional phrase beginning with the preposition *of*. The effects of this structure are twofold: similar or parallel structures give rhythm to the prose and the postmodification using other nouns adds emphasis by drawing out the phrase This is especially true of the final example.

2. Noun phrases that you should have identified for their pre- and/or postmodification are the following:

    the swaying crowd in the station at the North Wall
    soldiers with brown baggages
    the wide doors of the sheds
    a glimpse of the black mass of the boat
    the quay wall
    illumined portholes
    her cheek pale and cold
    a maze of distress
    a long mournful whistle
    a nausea in her body

Pre- and postmodification extend the noun phrase, and in each of this case what's added is not just clarification but significant detail. You might argue that the sentences containing these phrases are longer than strictly necessary, and they may have the effects of suspension, intensity and emphasis.

3. The word *sea(s)* in a noun phrase is found in the story as follows:

    (on) the sea, all the seas of the world, (amid) the seas

There's something slightly odd about these phrases: one is 'at sea', not 'on the sea', and the combination of determiner + plural noun adds to the implied enormity and threatening nature of the sea.

Exploring & Writing

Task A

1. Here are three important events:

    trip
    wedding
    fire

2. In the following, the nouns are developed into pre- and postmodified noun phrases:

    the once-in-a lifetime, crazily adventurous, round-the world <u>trip</u> that taught us a lot about the world
    the glamorously extravagant <u>wedding</u> of my best friend from school
    the devastating wild <u>fire</u> that wiped out the entire forest

3. With so much information surrounding the missing head nouns the words should be easy to guess.

Task B

1. In the following three examples we used premodification, postmodification, and both pre- and postmodification respectively:

    an impassioned, blinding, unconditional, unrequited, crazy, stupid, young <u>love</u>
    [the] <u>sorrow</u> that followed the tragic death of her colleague whose injuries were above the best doctors' immense knowledge and experience and beyond the state-of-the art equipment of the new hospital
    the enormous, bright-red, exotic-looking, totally delicious <u>tomato</u> that I picked from the market on my way back home from work at the end of my shift yesterday afternoon

2. You might have found that too many premodifying adjectives ran the risk of near-overlap or straightforward repetition; or that a seemingly endless postmodification exhausts the audience. Writers know when to stop. Additional information may add suspense, exaggeration or elegance, but too much of it will have a negative effect.

Task C

1. This is going to be the story of a young woman who can't decide whether to call her partner immediately or wait until the next day.

2. The opening sentence would consist of:
Letter + awaited her.

Suggested Answers

3. The essence of the plot is that she is upset and can't decide what to do because she doesn't understand the letter he had written to her.

4. Let's add pre- and postmodification:
A handwritten <u>letter</u> on the mantelpiece awaited her.

5. 'A handwritten letter (on the mantelpiece)' could be reworked into a new noun phrase, *'a handwriting that was familiar'*.

6-8. This is the paragraph, with both phrases included:
A handwritten letter on the mantelpiece awaited her. 'Alice', the envelope simply said, the handwriting at once familiar and strange. She opened the letter. Had it been earlier in the day she might have read it through and called him by telephone, but by now, with the sun low in the sky, she knew he would be too drunk. It was a waste. She would leave it. Tomorrow she could call from work. But what if it were not a bluff? What if the letter's threats this time were true? She read it again. Something in the tone marked it out as different. Something seemed more reconciled or deliberate, more coherent and determined. She thought of the seasons that had passed since they first met and picked up the phone.

Nouns and noun phrases contain the themes of the narrative, and the audience's attention would be drawn to the most frequent ones. The head nouns *letter* and *phone* are key, and as we see the character is torn between the two. The way these keywords are described (by modification as well as other lexical or syntactic means) is also significant. Notice, for instance, that the letter is handwritten yet the writing seems odd; as if to match its ominous content.

Task D

Hemingway's *Hills Like White Elephants* uses 'the hills' as a repeated motif. (The hills and the white elephants are of course symbolic of the central topic of the story, so do read the text if you can access it!) The noun phrase 'the hills' is seemingly simple, determiner + head noun; but it is always 'the' hills, specific, magnificent and attention-seeking. Less imposing objects are no less significant in the narrative, as we see with the beer motif: *beer..., two glasses of beer..., the beer glasses..., his beer..., the beer..., another beer.*

Review & Reflection

Task A

'Eveline' as head noun, with pre- and/or postmodification:
 Eveline in love.
 Eveline who will be trapped into a marriage of convenience.
 Young, optimistic Eveline who was about to leave Dublin.
 Anxious Eveline with a hard decision to make.

Task B

Each phrase above reveals something different about Eveline. This reflects the changing perspective of the narrative. But you may find working in your work that some readers saw more than was explicitly or implicitly suggested by the story!

Task C

It is the case that heavy noun modification may not be desirable and may even be unintentionally amusing.

The black and white stripy zebra walked across the green grass in the hot African sun

Everybody knows what a zebra looks like so there's no need to state the obvious. Also, the definite article seems to specify one zebra out of many, so the colour adjective is the wrong choice anyway as it does nothing further to specify which zebra. 'Stripy' is odd too as it duplicates 'black and white' and both are widely known features. Similarly, 'green' also seems superfluous, and while the' African sun' is evocative, the 'hot African sun' leaves little to the imagination.

I went to a party where I met a woman whose daughter knows my mother who you saw the day when we met where we usually go.

In theory, we can continue the sentence interminably (through a process called recursion, which allows for an infinite number of complement clauses to be used repeatedly in sequence). In practice, however, readers will sooner or later to lose track of the main focus of the sentence.

Task D

Noun phrases can be modified for a range of effects: new information, revelation, emphasis, exaggeration, suspense, intrigue, or to simply lengthen the prose to better capture a lingering action or an intense thought. Repeated noun phrases can act as motifs in a narrative which can cause readers to ponder on points of similarity.

Chapter 4

Verbs 1: Tense and Aspect

Textual Analysis of the Narrative

Task A

The verbs are underlined below:

One time there <u>used</u> <u>to be</u> a field there
They <u>used to play</u> every evening with other people's children

Suggested Answers   135

Then a man from Belfast <u>bought</u> the field and <u>built</u> houses in it
Her father <u>used</u> often <u>to hunt</u> them in out of the field
Now she <u>was going to go away</u> like the others

Task B

1. '*Now*' in the narrative can mean the present, the past or the future, depending on its position in the narrative and whose perspective we are invited to adopt.

   Now she was going to go away: from Eveline's point of view, this is in the future.

   He is in Melbourne now: direct speech belonging to Eveline's father; 'now' would be contemporary to the time the father spoke these words; from Eveline's point of view, this is in the past.

   Even now, though she was over nineteen: from Eveline's point of view, this is in the present moment.
2. Most verbs in the second paragraph are in the past tense.
3. One verb is in a different tense: *Everything <u>changes</u>.*
4. The present tense shows the universality and timelessness of the statement, as if independent from the completed events described in the paragraph.

Task C

1. The narration is written in past tense; direct speech is given in the present tense.
2. Direct speech brings the character to life; the present tense helps us readers see and hear what is happening at a specific point in the narrative, as if we were live witnesses.

Task D

1. The first phrase combines the past simple (*She <u>looked</u> round the room*) with the past perfect *(she <u>had dusted</u> once a week for so many years)*. The use of the past perfect form places the action of dusting further in the past and, in 'combination with 'for so many years', emphasises the regularity and repetitiveness of the action, right up to the point that 'she looked around'.
2. Other examples that combine the past simple and the past perfect are the following:

   Tizzie Dunn <u>was</u> dead, too, and the Waters <u>had gone</u> back to England.
   [What would they say of her in the Stores] when they <u>found out</u> that she <u>had run away</u> with a fellow?
   She knew it <u>was</u> that that <u>had given</u> her the palpitations.
   How well she <u>remembered</u> the first time she <u>had seen</u> him...
   He <u>told</u> her the names of the ships he <u>had been</u> on and the names of the different services.
   Ernest <u>had been</u> her favourite but she <u>liked</u> Harry too.

The contrast gives a sense of layers of time: the reader knows what happened first and what later. It's also useful in showing perspective: the narration is in the past simple and focuses on Eveline. Eveline's past with all the characters involved, filtered through her memory, is shown in the past perfect for a distancing effect. In all but the last example, use of the past perfect allows the action which occurred first (in the sequence of two actions) to be reported last. This also has the effect of emphasising how Eveline's present in the story is anchored by events in a deeper past.

Task E

1. The verb form 'went' is of course simple past, but *if + simple past* is a conditional, indicating a hypothetical action.
2. The verbs are all in the past, the past tense is most used in the narrative and the simple aspect on this occasion downplays the duration of Eveline's hardship, and we are invited to see that from her point of view. The adverbial 'now' is a narrative technique that places the event firmly in the present moment, again from the protagonist's perspective.
3. Another instance of this technique is: *And now she had nobody to protect her.* See also B1 above.

Task F

1. In the third paragraph, the narration is in the past tense. Things referring to Eveline's past previous to the moment being described are in the past perfect. This creates effects similar to those described in Task D2 above.
2. The changing aspect (from simple to perfect) indicates the sequence of events and the progression of time. (Again, see D2 above.)
3. Phrases like *during all those years, another day, one day, then, not long before, afterwards* help set the narrative in the past. These phrases have the same function as adverbs; conveniently they are called adverbials to reflect exactly that function (see Chap. 6 for more on adverbials.)

Task G

1. Interrogatives are found in the story as follows:

   Was that wise?
   What would they say of her in the Stores when they found out that she had run away with a fellow?
   "Miss Hill, don't you see these ladies are waiting?"
   Why should she be unhappy?
   Could she still draw back after all he had done for her?

With the exception of the direct speech, the interrogatives belong to Eveline's internal speech; immersed in her thought, she is pondering or interrogating herself.

Suggested Answers 137

2. Imperatives are found in the story as follows:

> "Look lively, Miss Hill, please."
> Escape! She must escape!
> "Come!"

The two in direct speech are addressed to Eveline (the former a recollection of an interaction at work, the latter from the 'live scene' at the port, where Frank is calling her to board the ship). *Escape!* could be the voice in Eveline's head, or the narrator instigating a strong emotion. *She must escape!* is more indirect, as if the narrator/reader felt the urge to cry at the protagonist.

3. Interrogatives and imperatives bring the characters to life. It's as if the narrator steps back and lets the characters do the talking.

Exploring & Writing

Task A

1. Here is a possible narrative:

    She is married. She is unhappy. She meets a stranger. She falls in love. She discovers a dark secret.

2. Alternative versions:

    a) *She meets a stranger. She falls in love. She is married. She discovers a dark secret. She is unhappy.*
    b) *She meets a stranger. She discovers a dark secret. She is unhappy. She falls in love. She is married.*

    There is probably some logic in any ordering you may imagine!

3. In the past tense:

    She was married. She was unhappy. She met a stranger. She fell in love. She discovered a dark secret.

4. Changing tense and/or aspect:

    She had been married (for years). She had been unhappy (all those years). (Then) she met a stranger. She is now falling in love (but) she will discover a dark secret.

5. You may like the fast pace of the story in 3, but the version in 4 gives a better sense of sequence and duration: of the length of her marriage and the period she had been unhappy, which are contrary to the sudden, quick encounter with the stranger. The reader also knows what is happening in the present moment and gets a hint about things to come. That way the narrative also builds up a sense of anticipation.

Task B

1. Author A will talk about his wedding day.
2. Here are in ingredients:

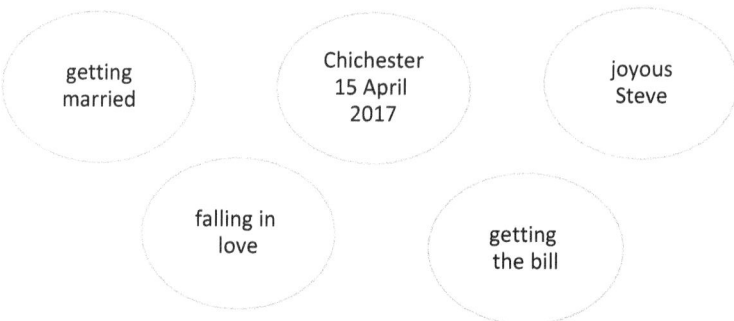

3. Here is what author B came up, using the circles above:

   On April 15, 2017, in Chichester, he got married to the woman he had fallen in love with a short while before. In one word, it was a joyous event. His best friend Steve looked especially joyous, but all the guests seemed to enjoy themselves. Receiving the bill once the party was over was not as joyous though.

4. There are issues with what author B wrote: how long before the wedding had A fallen in love? Who is Steve? When did A receive the bill?

5. Adding interrogatives and imperatives:

   On April 15, 2017, in Chichester, he got married to the woman he had fallen in love with a short while before. In one word, it was a joyous event. His best friend Steve looked especially joyous. Was he drunk? In any case all the guests seemed to enjoy themselves. Receiving the bill once the party was over isn't going to be as joyous though. Steve, lend him some money!

6. Comments about changes in 5:

   B wrote his narrative in the past tense. Adding an interrogative could have been an opportunity to introduce direct speech, though free indirect speech (still in third person narration, but the question lessening the distance between the event, the narrator and the reader) was chosen instead. Imperatives are normally uttered in the here and now, demanding action in the immediate future. This is why the preceding verb couldn't be in the past tense.

7. Here is original narrative written by A. Note the first-person narrative; this is now entirely his point of view and describes the events as they actually took place.

   'The will to love, and then the bill'
   We married, and not on any old day, but on Easter Saturday, 15 April 2017. And not in any old place, but in ancient Chichester. This date and place, as my friend Steve remarked, made for the most joyous of occasions. Falling in love

Suggested Answers   139

had led to this, just as winter had led to spring. Afterwards, there was the bill, so others were happy too.

8. In summary, verbs tell about events. They contain information about what happens, when it happens, the duration of the action or event, and, in text, the sequence of events. They may be statements, orders or questions.

Task C

You'll find that most short narratives are narrated in the simple past tense, from a third-person objective perspective. Dialogue or monologue in direct speech are then often used to break up the narrative, bringing the characters to life. In these shorter parts you find a variety of perspectives, and reference to events that appear to take place in the here and now of the characters' lives, or refer to the future, etc. Differing tenses and aspects help achieve this layering of points of view, temporality and references to people, places and other events. Hemingway's *Hills Like White Elephants* is narrated in the third person, and the actions are placed in the past. The first paragraph describes the setting and is rich in imagery. All the verbs are in the past simple: *the hills were..., on this side there was..., the American and the girl sat..., it was very hot..., it [the train] stopped...* The last main paragraph is also in the past, but the aspect switches from simple to progressive: *he picked up the bags..., he looked up the tracks..., he walked through the barroom..., people were drinking..., he drank..., they were waiting... he went out..., she was sitting...* It's as if *he* moved quickly and did things, while *people/they* and *she* remained at their positions and carried on with what they had being doing for some time. It's possible that in this way Hemingway foregrounds the male character, while everybody else is pushed into the background.

Review & Reflection

Task A

The verbs are underlined below; the main verbs are in **bold**:

*Ernest had **been** her favourite but she **liked** Harry too.*

The first verb is in the past perfect; the second is in the past simple. We know from the story that Ernest had died, so the perfective aspect places the action further into the past. There is an implied sense that she liked Ernest the most for as long as he was alive.

Task B

	Simple	Continuous/progressive	Perfect	Perfect continuous/progressive
Present	changes	is changing	has changed	has been changing
Past	changed	was changing	had changed	had been changing

As we said in B4 of Textual analysis, the present simple indicates the universality and timelessness of the statement. It's a fact that's independent from the other events described in the paragraph. It's relevant to Eveline 'now', who is brought closer to us if we assume that the statement is given as a direct thought which, like direct speech, reduces the distance between the characters and the reader.

Task C

Storytelling is about events. It's the verbs that capture the essence of events, propelling the story forward, indicating to the reader what happened and when it happened. How things happened and who is involved in what happened are narrated by verb phrases in combination with other elements of the clause, as we shall examine in the following chapters.

Chapter 5

Verbs 2: Modality, Catenation, Multi-Word Verbs

Textual Analysis of the Narrative

Task A

1. The meaning of 'would' in the following phrases:

    *Perhaps she **would** never **see** again those familiar objects:* possibility
    *She **would not cry** many tears at leaving the Stores:* unwillingness
    *She **would not be treated** as her mother had been:* unwillingness or prediction
    *In the end he **would give** her the money:* habituality (given the reference to the past)
    *Frank **would save** her:* possibility (or willingness, or even hope or belief)

Clearly, some of the phrases potentially carry multiple interpretations.

2. In the following, 'would' is repeated several times:

    But in her new home, in a distant unknown country, it would not be like that. Then she would be married—she, Eveline. People would treat her with respect then. She would not be treated as her mother had been.

These lines represent Eveline's thoughts about her future, what would happen when she leaves the country. She speaks with a degree of certainty, though it might be just a strong desire for what she wishes or wants to happen.

3. The meanings of the modals in the following examples:

    She must escape!: necessity

Suggested Answers   141

> *Could she still draw back (after all he had done for her?):* willingness or possibility
> *Her promise to keep the home together as long as she could:* ability
> *He would save her:* possibility
> *Why should she be unhappy?:* duty or obligation

These phrases are from the point of view of Eveline: that *he would save her* might be a possibility unless she sees it as his duty to do so. The interrogatives are particularly tricky: *could she draw back?* implies she doesn't think it's the right thing to do, so to interpret the modal as 'ability' is a little vague. Similarly, *why should she be unhappy?* is a rhetorical question; it's as if she knows she is doomed to be unhappy but feels strongly that she doesn't deserve it.

4. Changing 'would' to 'must' gives an urgency about the future events, as if they can't happen any other way, and suggests an obligation or commitment for those involved:

> *But in her new home, in a distant unknown country, it must not be like that. Then she must be married—she, Eveline. People must treat her with respect then. She must not be treated as her mother had been.*

Changing 'would' to 'could' reduces the degree of possibility:

> *But in her new home, in a distant unknown country, it could not be like that. Then she could be married—she, Eveline. People could treat her with respect then. She could not be treated as her mother had been.*

Task B

1. The semi-modal 'used to' is used to refer to events from Eveline's childhood: *there used to be a field..., they used to play..., her father used often to hunt them..., Keogh used to keep nix...* None of that is true anymore because 'everything changes', as said later. The repetition emphasizes Eveline's varied and vivid memories, and gives a sense of nostalgia, of Eveline's longing for happier, more carefree times. 'Used to' also emphasises the regularity and repetition of the events and, at the same time, distances them from Eveline's present.
2. The subjects are indicated below:

> *(He) **used to** pass it with a casual word:* the father
> *He **used to** meet her outside the Stores every evening:* Frank
> *He **used to** call her Poppens:* Frank
> *(He) often **used to** hunt them in:* the father

All of these refer to habitual actions in the past.

Joyce causes Evelyn to use the same semi-modal to reflect on the actions of the two men, one she has known all her life and one she has met recently, perhaps to further emphasize the central theme of this story: Eveline is torn between her obligation towards her father that pulls her to stay put and the new adventure promised by

Frank that pushes her forward and away. For a large part of the story, these choices seem equally weighty for Eveline. The use of 'used to' to refer to Frank's more recent and limited actions (in contrast to those of her father) potentially also emphasises Eveline's desire for Frank to create for her the sense of stability and 'anchoring' once provided for her by her family. They also indicate to the reader the sense that Eveline sees Frank as a potential positive substitute father-figure who will take care of her.

Task C

1. Joyce's use of the marginal modal 'be about to' creates a sense of anticipation for what will happen in the very near future: *She was about to leave it..., She was about to explore another life....*

    The events are imminent, pressing even, and this sense of urgency will come to a climax when Eveline is overwhelmed by her inability to move.
2. Similarly, the marginal modal 'be going to' indicates events that will happen soon and with relative certainty. *She was going to go away* appears at the beginning of the story and this is what we need to know about Eveline at this point. *He said he wasn't going to give her his hard-earned money* appears later on in the narrative, as Eveline recollects events and words from the past. We can assume that what is said about the father happened regularly, and that the force of his words is still fresh in her memory.
3. In short, the semi-modals highlight the immediacy and urgency of the events described, all of which propel the story to the final resolution. That the story ends with barely a 'resolution' but rather with Eveline's paralysis, mirrors the tension felt through the narrative, and emphasizes the contrast between future prospects and the present that's come to a halt.

Task D

1. In the following, the catenated verbs are underlined:

    i. *She <u>continued to sit</u> by the window*
    ii. *He <u>took her to see</u> the Bohemian Girl*
    iii. *But she <u>wanted to live</u>*
    iv. *She <u>was to go away</u> with him by the night boat <u>to be</u> his wife and <u>to live</u> with him in Buenos Ayres*
    v. *They <u>had come to know</u> each other*
    vi. *Still they <u>seemed to have been</u> rather happy then*
    vii. *Her father ... <u>had forbidden her to have</u> anything <u>to say</u> to him*

2. The narrative emphasises those things that have begun to change for Eveline, which cumulatively would lead up to biggest change of all, her departure from Dublin. The regular use of catenated phrases, however, also emphasises that nothing is simple of certain for Eveline, e.g. she didn't live, but she wanted to

Suggested Answers

live. The lengthening of the phases via catenation also distances Eveline from the actions and so makes them seem more tentative and uncertain.
3. We might argue that characters engage in actions which in turn prompt other characters to engage in other actions. They are in this way not only active but effective upon the behaviour of others. For example, *Her father ... had forbidden her to have anything to say to him* means that an action instigated by the father made the daughter alter her behaviour. They also show the strong interconnections of the characters.
4. A simple, lexical verb denotes a straightforward action, like in this example referring to Eveline's father: "*I know these sailor chaps," he said.* But things aren't as simple for Eveline: *she was going to go away..., she would never see again..., She had consented to go away..., she would be married..., she had nobody to protect her..., she had to rush out as quickly..., she was about to leave it..., she was about to explore...., she was to go away...., she had to meet her lover secretly..., she wanted to live...* Examples like these indicate the uncertainty of what was happening and what was to come. As in the printed version, the subject is some distance from the main verb rather than immediately preceding it, so Eveline is depicted as detached from her actions, perhaps feeling out of control.

Task E

1. Explanation of multi-word verbs:

    The Waters *had **gone back*** to England = returned
    They found out that she *had **run away*** with a fellow = escape
    Her place *would be **filled up*** by advertisement = taken
    He *had* never ***gone for*** her = attacked
    He ***read*** her ***out*** a ghost story = read
    Her time *was **running out*** = expiring
    *Could she still **draw back** after all he had done for her?* = withdraw

2. Joyce uses multi-word verbs perhaps for the same reason that such verbs are generally more frequently used than their single-word equivalents. They are made up of simple Anglo-Saxon words, whereas the alternatives would be more complex Latinate words. They keep up the pace and help the prose flow. Their colloquial flavour thus adds authenticity to Eveline's voice.

Exploring & Writing

Task A

1. The initial statements:

    I completed 20 marathons
    I won at a poetry competition.

2. With modal verbs and catenative verbs respectively:

   I might have completed 20 marathons. I attempted to complete 20 marathons. I should have won at a poetry competition. I wanted to win at a poetry competition.

3. The statements in 2 either negate or cast doubt on the statements in 1: *I might have completed 20 marathons* means *I'm not sure, I haven't counted. I attempted to complete* implies that *I tried but didn't make it in the end. I should have won* means *I haven't actually won. I wanted to win* also suggests *I probably didn't win.*

Task B

1. The chosen tale is *The Hen that Laid Golden Eggs,* one of Aesop's fables.
2. Here is the story:

   A man had a hen who laid a golden egg every day. One day he had the idea that the hen would have some great treasure inside, and he caught her and slaughtered her to find treasure in her womb. All he found were common hen's insides, and the hen was no longer alive to lay a golden egg every day.

3. With changed verb forms, as instructed:

   A man used to have a hen who could lay a golden egg every day. One day he had the idea that the hen would have some great treasure inside, and he wanted to catch her and slaughter her to find treasure in her womb. All he should find would be common hen's insides, and the hen would no longer be alive to lay a golden egg every day.

4. The changes actually alter the story: That he *wanted to catch it* doesn't mean he actually did it., which is confirmed by the modal formations that follow.

Task C

1. The story above, from the perspective of the man:

   I had a hen who laid a golden egg every day. One day I had the idea that the hen would have some great treasure inside, and I caught her and slaughtered her to find treasure in her womb. Alas! All I found were common hen's insides, and the hen was no longer alive to lay a golden egg every day.

2. The first-person perspective works surprisingly well! But Aesop's tales were always in third person, always told by an omnipresent narrator who saw and knew everything!

Review & Reflection

Task A

1. Single word verb, past simple declarative: *had (shelter and food)*
2. Verb with an auxiliary verb to form past perfect simple: *had dusted*
3. Verb with an auxiliary verb to form past continuous: *were courting*

Suggested Answers

4. Interrogative verb (present simple): *don't you see?*
5. Single word verb, imperative: *come!*
6. Verb with modal verb: *must escape*
7. Verb with semi-modal: *was about to leave (it)*
8. Verb with catenation: *continued to sit*
9. Verb with past simple multi-word verb: *found out*

Task B

1.	Simple present verb: *I write*	Verb with a modal: *I could write*
2.	Present perfect verb: *I have written*	Verb with a multi-word verb: *I'm writing up (sth)*
3.	Verb with catenation: *I wanted to write*	Simple past verb: *I wrote*
4.	Imperative verb: *Write!*	Past continuous verb: *I was writing*
5.	Past perfect verb: *I had written*	Verb with a semi-modal: *I used to write*
6.	Interrogative verb: *Do you write?*	Past perfect continuous verb: *I had been writing*

Task C

1. Some of the grammatical concepts covered by Chaps. 4 and 5 might have been familiar to you already, but we hope that including them here has helped you not only revise the terminology, but also see these grammatical categories in context, understand their function, and assess the effects of their use in narratives.
2. Verbs in general are significant because they contain information about what happens (internally or externally) and about events, feelings and experience. From what we have studied so far, mood and modality are possibly the most important aspect in Joyce's narrative, and in grammar in general. They change the meaning of the verb from simply empirical, to relational and evaluative. In other words, verbs don't just signify actions, but they also assess them and/or create stances on them (and those involved with them).

Chapter 6

Verb Phrases

Textual Analysis of the Narrative

Task A

1. He <u>said</u> she used to squander the money
It <u>was</u> hard work
Then she <u>had</u> to rush out
In the end he would <u>give</u> her the money

2. Transitive verb = squander; ditransitive verb = give; intransitive verb = rush (out); copular verb = was
3. Own words:

> People would respect her.
> Ernest had died.
> Harry was away.

Actual words:

> People would treat her with respect.
> Ernest was dead.
> Harry was nearly always down somewhere in the country.

Comparison: The first example had verb + object + prepositional phrase; we changed it to verb + object. The second example had copular verb + complement; we changed to intransitive verb. The third example had verb + adverbial; we changed the adverbial.

4. The type of complements a verb can take is often determined by the meaning of the verb. For example, 'give' is begging for 'what?' or 'to whom'? 'die' needs nothing to be added, other than perhaps information about the place or the manner, i.e. an adverbial.

Task B

1. *Eveline was tired*
Her father was not so bad then
Eveline would be married
Her father was usually fairly bad on Saturday night
Frank was very kind, manly, open-hearted
Eveline felt elated as she sat in an unaccustomed part of the theatre
Frank was awfully fond of music
Her father was becoming old lately
Her father could be very nice

2. The verb phrases above are formed of copular verbs + complements; each phrase reveals something about the characters involved.
3. The father's character is framed chronologically, e.g. he was not so bad then, indeed he could be nice sometimes, he is pretty bad now, and he is getting old. Frank is in the present and the future, kind and open-hearted and a potential saviour. Eveline is torn between the reality and the prospect of an alternative life, and he get to observe her internal world as she is reminiscing her past by the window, imagining the future as she sits alone in the room in the evening, or she is waiting to embark the ship at the docks.

Suggested Answers 147

4. The copular verbs are underline below:

   That <u>was</u> a long time ago; she and her brothers and sisters <u>were</u> all grown up her mother <u>was</u> dead.
   Ernest <u>was</u> dead and Harry, who <u>was</u> in the church decorating business, <u>was</u> nearly always down somewhere in the country.
   The station <u>was</u> full of soldiers with brown baggages.

   Through these sentences, we move from familiar characters, then and now, to the present situation, and the mass crowd of soldiers. The heavy use of copular verbs also creates an overall feeling of stasis; of characters who simply 'are' rather than those who have great agency.

5. *Why should she be unhappy?* is an interesting rhetorical question. It reveals Eveline's state in the present but also interrogates it, almost suggesting there could be an alternative.

   Joyce often uses copular verb phrases to describe minor characters (around the three main characters) as they have no agency in the narrative, e.g. *He is in Melbourne now.*

Task C

1. *he had never gone for her:* subject is the father, object is Eveline
   he would give her the money: subject is the father, indirect object is Eveline, direct object is the money
   he took her to see the Bohemian Girl: subject is Frank, object is Eveline
   he would save her: subject is Frank, object is Eveline
   he held her hand: subject is Frank, object is Eveline, i.e. 'her hand'
   he had done for her: subject is Frank, object is Eveline
   he would drown her: subject is frank, object is Eveline

2. The verbs above reveal an action initiated by the father or Frank, with Eveline always on the receiving end. Cumulatively, they show us the impact the two men have on Eveline's life and how little agency Eveline assumes for her own life
3. The two men are involved in physical action; Eveline often suffers as the result of the action, whether it is positive or negative.
4. In the sentence *her father had found out the affair and had forbidden her to have anything to say to him* the father is again in the subject position, initiator of the actions of finding out and forbidding; *the affair* and *her* are both direct objects.

   In the sentence *he had quarrelled with Frank* 'he', the father, is the subject; interestingly there's no direct object; Frank is part of the adverbial, i.e. involved in the action in a different way, implying the action wouldn't have taken place without him.

Task D

1. The adverbials are underlined below:

   <u>In her home</u> anyway she had shelter and food = place
   she had dusted <u>once a week for so many years</u> = time
   <u>During all those years</u> she had never found out the name of the priest = time
   She stood up <u>in a sudden impulse of terror</u> = manner
   <u>Through the wide doors of the sheds</u> she caught a glimpse = place
   The boat blew a long mournful whistle <u>into the mist</u> = place
   He rushed <u>beyond the barrier</u> = place

2. Examples 1, 3 and 5 unusually begin with adverbials of place. Both adverbials of place and time can be 'fronted', for emphasis.
3. Balanced clauses of equal length and similar structure contribute to the rhythm of the text.
4. The clauses towards the end of the narrative are not even so the text does not display a similar rhythmic quality. This perhaps emphasises the content. Also, the places in 3 above are all nearby and physical, whereas the places in the prepositional phrases towards the end of the text are more distant e.g. *into the mist,* or refer to Eveline's own body as if she is retreating into herself and away from worlds that might be. The emphasis is therefore different.

Task E

1. In terms of content, long adverbials add more detail; in terms of style, they vary the rhythm and pace of the text. They also emphasise the significant of place and time in the narrative; Eveline is, in a sense, ensnared by familiar places and memories.
2. The adverbials describe what Eveline is looking at from the window in great detail. Readers can almost see the scenes themselves. Also, this is a good example of 1 above.
3. The beginning and the end are most dense with adverbials. At the beginning, readers need the details to paint the picture of Eveline and her surroundings. At the end, details are also important, but the long descriptions also prolong the prose, giving a sense of anticipation in a part of the narrative that is full of intensity.

Exploring & Writing

Task A

1. Let's work with *they met secretly.*
2. With adverbials: *For months, they met secretly in a supermarket car park.*
3. With further additions, as instructed:

Suggested Answers 149

    i. *Daily for months, they met secretly in a supermarket car park.*
    ii. *Almost daily for months, they met secretly in a supermarket car park.*
    iii. *Almost daily for months, they met secretly in an out-of-town supermarket car park.*
    iv. *Almost daily for months, madly in love, they met secretly in an out-of-town supermarket car park.*
    v. *Almost daily for months, madly in love, they met secretly in an out-of-town supermarket car park to kiss in the dark.*
    vi. *Madly in love, almost daily for months, they met secretly in an out-of-town supermarket car park to kiss in the dark.*

4. This one seems to work, but most would agree that some details are more significant than others. There is also a sense in which 'the meeting' becomes eclipsed by too much additional information.
5. In theory there are no limits. But readers can only process a certain amount of information, and writers may choose to put emphasis on the manner or the place etc. but not all aspects at once as it becomes difficult for readers to discern the main focus of the text

Task B

1. i. *He rushed beyond the barrier and called to her to follow.*
Changing the adverbial of place: *He rushed past the blockade and called to her to follow.*
ii. *He was shouted at to go on but he still called to her.*
Making the verb in the second verb phrase ditransitive: *He was shouted at to go on but he still sent her a signal of embrace.*
iii. *She set her white face to him, passive, like a helpless animal.*
Changing the verb. *She turned her white face to him, passive, like a helpless animal.*
iv. *Her eyes gave him no sign of love or farewell or recognition.*
Changing the verb from ditransitive to transitive. *Her eyes showed no sign of love or farewell or recognition.*

2. Verb transitivity alters the information that follows the verb; in examples ii and iv above it was hard, for example, to change the verb from transitive to ditransitive without altering the content slightly. Examples i and iii are also hard to change: 'blockade' and 'turned' work, but they affect the narrative by introducing tones not in the original. 'Blockade' carries the idea of a barrier designed to restrict transit and 'turned' ascribes more agency to Eveline than the original 'set'. Trying to alter elements of a text is often a useful way to appreciate the impacts and craft of the original author.

Task C

1. 'I often seem absent-minded and preoccupied. In truth, I become completely oblivious to everything and everybody around me. I feel happy in my thoughts. I am just a day-dreamer.'
2. 'I close my eyes. I am lying on a turquoise beach. I hear exotic birds and the sound of the waves. I get up and pick up the surfboard and run into the sea. I'm now catching the biggest waves and I am winning.'
3. and 4. The first paragraph reveals a person totally preoccupied with their internal world. Both the words and the grammar are used to express that. There are no actions, just states. With the second paragraph the writer redeems herself: she may be dreaming, but at least her actions are real and quite adventurous; there is a sense of the protagonist shaping her world

Review & Reflection

Task A

1. A copular verb: *He <u>had been</u> a school friend of her father.*
A transitive verb: *she had never <u>found out</u> the name of the priest*
A ditransitive verb: *he <u>showed</u> the photograph to a visitor*
An adverbial describing pace: *She looked <u>round the room</u>.*
An adverbial referring to time: *she dusted <u>once a week</u>*

2. Complements are direct and indirect objects for transitive verbs, subject and object complements for copular verbs. Adjuncts are adverbs or prepositional phrases, conveniently called adverbials.
3. Everything! Verb phrases are the most fundamental syntactic category in English structure.

Task B

The issue of transitivity is fundamental in every narrative including Joyce's *Eveline*. Examining the transitive verbs and their subjects and objects helps us understand what is happening and who is involved. At a deeper level, it helps us understand the characters themselves, the dynamic between them, the effect their behaviour has on each other. Also worthy of note in 'Eveline' is Joyce's use of copular verb phrases to contract with transitive and ditransitive phrases. These emphasise Eveline's own lack of agency in her world.

Suggested Answers

Chapter 7

Basic Clauses

Textual Analysis of the Narrative

Task A

1. *It was hard work:* It = subject; was hard work = predicate
The evening deepened in the avenue: The evening = subject; deepened in the avenue = predicate
Her distress awoke a nausea in her body: Her distress = subject; awoke a nausea in her body = predicate

2. *She <u>stood</u> among the swaying crowd in the station at the North Wall.*
All the seas of the world <u>tumbled</u> about her heart.
Her hands <u>clutched</u> the iron in frenzy.
Her eyes <u>gave</u> him no sign of love or farewell or recognition.

3. *Through the wide doors of the sheds she caught a glimpse of the black mass of the boat*
Subject of this clause = she
Predicate = caught a glimpse of the black mass of the boat
Clause with a similar structure = *Amid the seas she sent a cry of anguish.*
Placing the subject later in the clauses gives a sense of suspension of the theme, increasing the effect of anticipation on the reader's part.

Task B

1. The structure is Subject + Verb + Adverbial.
2. *She knew the air. Frank would save her.* Both have the structure Subject + Verb + Object
    Simple structures like this make for short sentences, which can be quite sharp and powerful. In a varied prose style, they demand attention in a different way. We only focus on the action and those involved.

Task C

1. The complements are underlined below:
    i. *That was a long time ago; she and her brothers and sisters were <u>all grown up</u> her mother was <u>dead</u>.* (both subject complements)
    ii. *It was hard work—a hard life—but now that she was about to leave it she did not find it <u>a wholly undesirable life</u>.* (object complement)
    iii. *The station was <u>full of soldiers with brown baggages</u>.* (subject complement)

2. *She set her white face to him, passive, like a helpless animal.*
   The underlined could describe her (subject), her white face (direct object), or even him (Frank) (indirect object). We find this a very clever and haunting image precisely because of the ambiguity in its complementization.

Task D

1. Clause structures:

    i. *She was tired.* = Subject + (Copular) Verb + Complement
    ii. *Everything changes.* = Subject + Verb
    iii. *She stood up in a sudden impulse of terror.* = Subject + Verb + Adverbial
    iv. *He would save her.* = Subject + Verb + Object
    v. *The station was full of soldiers with brown baggages.* = Subject + Copular Verb + Complement
    vi. *She answered nothing.* = Subject + Verb + Object
    vii. *The boat blew a long mournful whistle into the mist.* Subject + Verb + Object + Adverbial
    viii. *Her hands clutched the iron in frenzy.* Subject + Verb + Object + Adverbial

2. The last part of the narrative has the greatest concentration of sentences with a single clause. This is because they give a sense of speed. Things are happening in quick succession, time is running out, and Eveline has to make her mind up.

Exploring & Writing

Task A

1. He smiled.
She liked him.
She felt excited.
He went near her.
He gave her a kiss.
It made her happy.
She squeezed him in her arms.

2. The structures above are:
Subject + Verb
Subject + Verb + Object
Subject + Verb + Complement
Subject + Verb + Adverbial
Subject + Verb + Object (indirect) + Object (direct)
Subject + Verb + Object + Complement
Subject + Verb + Objcct + Adverbial

Suggested Answers   153

Task B

1. 'Ships at a distance have every man's wish on board'
Subject + Verb + Object + Adverbial
'All stories are love stories.'
Subject + Copular Verb + Complement
They both work because they are short, to the point, read like aphorisms, and invite you to read on.

2. 'The visitor arrived at midnight.'
3. We think this works because 'the visitor' is yet unidentified so you have to keep reading; 'at midnight' is mysterious enough', but at what sort of place do you arrive at midnight? Again, you need to keep reading. It's a single-clause sentence (Subject + Verb + Adverbial) that's both intriguing and simple.

Task C

1. Hemingway's Hills like White Elephants begins like this:

   The hills across the valley of the Ebro were long and white. On this side there was no shade and no trees and the station was between two lines of rails in the sun. Close against the side of the station there was the warm shadow of the building and a curtain, made of strings of bamboo beads, hung across the open door into the bar, to keep out flies. The American and the girl with him sat at a table in the shade, outside the building. It was very hot and the express from Barcelona would come in forty minutes. It stopped at this junction for two minutes and went on to Madrid.

   Clause structures:

   i. *The hills across the valley of the Ebro were long and white.* = Subject + Copular verb + Complement
   ii. *the station was between two lines of rails in the sun.* = Subject + Verb + Adverbial
   iii. *The American and the girl with him sat at a table in the shade, outside the building.* = Subject + Verb + Adverbials
   iv. *the express from Barcelona would come in forty minutes.* = Subject + Verb + Adverbial

   The first paragraph contains balanced clauses, some of very similar structure. There are fronted adverbials of place which, combined with other adverbials, add detail to this detailed descriptive part.

2. The very last sentences of the story are quite different: *"I feel fine," she said. "There's nothing wrong with me. I feel fine."* The story starts with a description of the scene and ends with the characters talking. The language is more casual, the sentences very short, and we are left to ponder on what the words mean. Compare this to a movie: long shots give you a bird's eye view of what's there; close-ups are all about the people and their words or expressions.

Task D

1. The poem might have inspired Joyce. there's certainly an overlap in the name and certain themes, such as the disapproval of their runaway marriage by family and society, and the shame the young women might feel as a result.
2. White snow covered the narrow pathway. The Lord of the Valley crossed over the moor. His deep footprints on the white snow showed his track to Eveleen's door. The sunrays of the next day melted away the footprints. The light above will remove the stain on Eveline's fame.
3. The clause structures, in the order they appear are:

    Subject + Verb + Object
    Subject + Verb + Adverbial
    Subject + Verb + Object
    Subject + Verb + Object
    Subject + Verb + Object

4–5. There are certainly issues with the structure above. Talking in basic clauses only isn't quite so natural. In the next chapter we look at how clauses combine to form more elaborate sentences.

Review & Reflection

Task A

Here is a summary of Chap. 7, in conjunction with Chap. 6:

Clause = Subject + Complement
Complement = Verb Phrase
Verb Phrase = Verb + Complement(s) + Adjunct(s)
Complements = Direct and Indirect Objects / Complements for copular verbs
Adjuncts = Adverbs / Prepositional Phrases (Adverbials)

Therefore, the 7 clause structures:

Subject + Verb
Subject + Verb + Object
Subject + Verb + Complement
Subject + Verb + Adverbial
Subject + Verb + Object (indirect) + Object (direct)
Subject + Verb + Object + Complement
Subject + Verb + Object + Adverbial

Suggested Answers

Task B

Joyce makes use of all clause structures, but the structure Subject + Verb (+ Object) + Adverbial seems to stand out. Attention is drawn to details about thoughts, behaviours and actions, and these are usually details about time, place, and manner.

Chapter 8

Sentences

Textual Analysis of the Narrative

Task A

1. i. *Her time was running out but she continued to sit by the window.* = compound sentence
(*Her time was running out* = coordinate clause / *but she continued to sit by the window* = coordinate clause)
ii. *She remembered the last night of her mother's illness.* = single clause = simple sentence
iii. *As she mused the pitiful vision of her mother's life laid its spell on the very quick of her being.* = compound sentence
(*as she mused* = subordinate clause / *the pitiful vision of her mother's life laid its spell on the very quick of her being* = main clause)

2. Simple sentence = *She was tired.*
Compound sentence = *Her head was leaned against the window curtains and in her nostrils was the odour of dusty cretonne.*
Complex sentence = *Another day, when their mother was alive, they had all gone for a picnic to the Hill of Howth.*

Task B

1. The compound sentence in A1 represents contrasting events. In A2 the sentence is a sequence of events.
2. The complex sentence in A1 represents two overlapping events. In A2 the function of the sentence is very similar, also representing two events; one is ongoing while the other punctuates it.

Task C

1. Of the four instances of 'but', only two are used the way we have discussed in this chapter, i.e. as a coordinating conjunction placed between to independent clauses to form a compound sentence. In one instance 'but' begins a sentence

and in another it follows a semi-colon. This isn't entirely incorrect though in some registers it is not advisable. In prose fiction it's absolutely fine! Joyce uses 'but' to a good effect, highlighting the contradictions that trouble his heroine.

2. *What would they say of her in the Stores/ when they found out/ that she had run away with a fellow?* There are three clauses in this sentence as marked. The complement clauses are *when they found out* and *that she had run away with a fellow*.

3. *People knew/ that they were courting/ and, when he sang about thee lass/ that loves a sailor/, she always felt pleasantly confused.* There are five clauses in this sentence as marked. The complement clauses are *that they were courting* (a verb complement of 'knew') and *that loves a sailor* (a noun complement of 'thee lass'). The whole sentence is compound-complex.

Task D

1. A combination of simple and compound sentences is found in the first paragraph (and throughout the narrative). The variety changes the pace of the piece. When Joyce wants us to observe things alongside or via Eveline, sentences are long and descriptive. Short, single-clause sentences are sharp and powerful or disturbing. They interrupt the flow of the longer sentences thus introducing a sense of disquiet.
2. The last paragraph is very similar to the beginning, but the rhythms of complex and compound sentences are 'disturbed' even more by short simple sentences
3. Other simple sentences: *She was tired. / Few people passed.* Short sentences are used in dialogue, but also when here is a contrast to be made, for example between a lingering thought and a matter-of-fact statement, or a prolonged description of a situation and a wish for urgent action.
4. The compound sentences describing life with Frank suggest that things between him and Eveline were quite simple and straightforward. Life was more complicated around her father, as indicated by more intricate, complex sentences, that signify time relations, contradictions, reasons and causes of events. We suggest this also emphasises that many of the descriptions of Frank are simply accounts of his past which he has reported to Eveline, whereas Eveline has lived the complexities of life with her father.

Exploring & Writing

Task A

1-4. Sarah loved Peter and Peter loved her back. (compound)
Sarah loved Peter until he cheated on her. (complex)
Sarah loved Peter after he got ill. (complex)
Sarah loved Peter but Peter loved Jess. (compound)
Sarah loved Peter although he cheated on her. (complex)

Sarah loved Peter so she moved in with him. (compound)
Sarah loved Peter because he was kind. (complex)
Sarah loved Peter yet she didn't tell him. (compound)
Sarah loved Peter whenever they separated. (complex)

5. You can reverse the order of clauses in both compound and complex sentences without changing the meaning; the only restriction is the position of the subordinating conjunction.

Task B

1. It was a bright cold day in April, and the clocks were striking thirteen. = *1984*, George Orwell (1949)
Life changes fast. = *The Year of Magical Thinking*, Joan Didion (2005)
It is a truth universally acknowledged, that a single man in possession of a good fortune, must be in want of a wife. = *Pride & Prejudice*, Jane Austen (1813)
As Gregor Samsa awoke one morning from uneasy dreams he found himself transformed in his bed into a gigantic insect. = *Metamorphosis*, Franz Kafka (1915)
Mrs Dalloway said she would buy the flowers herself. = *Mrs Dalloway*, Virginia Woolf (1925)
In my younger and more vulnerable years my father gave me some advice that I've been turning over in my mind ever since. = *The Great Gatsby*, F. Scott Fitzgerald (1925)
Call me Ishmael. *Moby-Dick*, Herman Melville (1851)

2. Orwell = compound sentence
Didion = simple sentence
Austen = complex sentence
Kafka = complex sentence
Woolf = complex sentence
Fitzgerald = complex sentence
Melville = simple sentence

3. They all work for different reasons and are some of our favourite novel openings. Simple sentences are sharp and powerful. Compound sentences can sometimes be quite dull, but Orwell chooses his words and concepts to a shocking effect. Complex sentences are intricate, packing in a lot of information, yet they are intriguing enough to make you read on.
4. 'I can't see.' This is a single-clause, simple sentence that's intriguing and suspenseful. Who says this? What can't they not see? Can they see at all? You must read on!

Task C

1. The visitor dropped his suitcase.
2. The visitor dropped his suitcase and collapsed on a seat.

3. Although nobody expected him, the visitor dropped his suitcase and collapsed on a seat.
4. Although nobody expected him, the visitor dropped his suitcase and collapsed on a seat. He didn't say his name.
5. Although nobody expected him, the visitor dropped his suitcase and collapsed on a seat. He didn't say his name when he was asked.
6. The additions put events in sequence, add contradictions and generally establish relationships between events and those involved.

Task D

Didion's *The year of Magical Thinking* begins with three simple sentences, one compound and one complex. The simple sentences have parallel structures, beginning 'Life changes…'. It ends with four simple sentences and one compound. There's more repetition there: 'He told me that', and 'he did say that' as the second of the coordinate clauses. Didion's prose is powerful, often full of tension and urgency, and the short sharp sentences help achieve this.

Review & Reflection

Task A

1. Eveline is the heroine of the narrative but she is not the narrator.
   Eveline is the main protagonist of the narrative although the narration is in third person.
   Frank who is mentioned throughout, has a more active role in the end.
2. In the order they appear: compound, complex, complex.

Task B

The statement is largely true. Even writers who have a tendency for short sentences don't avoid complex sentences. Semantically, they intricate the relationships between actions and states of affairs, e.g. by contrasting, comparing, contradicting, sequencing, explaining cause and effect, give a condition, etc. Stylistically, the vary the pace, add rhythm, delay the theme, and create a sense of anticipation or suspense.

Suggested Answers

Chapter 9

Connecting Ideas: Clauses Revisited

Textual Analysis of the Narrative

Task A

1. i. *She knew it was that <u>that</u> had given her the palpitations*
ii. *She had ... to see that the two young children <u>who</u> had been left to her charge went to school regularly and got their meals regularly*
iii. *She was to go away with him ... to live with him in Buenos Ayres <u>where</u> he had a home waiting for her.*
iv. *Another day, <u>when</u> their mother was alive*
2. When the complementizer refers to the object it can be omitted.
3. The complement clause is underlined below:

   And yet during all those years she had never found out the name of the priest <u>whose yellowing photograph hung on the wall above the broken harmonium beside the coloured print of the promises made to blessed Margaret Mary Alacoque</u>

   This sentence seems to carry on at length, each new piece of information complemented by new information; this is achieved by a combination of complement clauses and adverbials. It evokes the detailed and interrelated information Eveline has accumulated about her home.

Task B

1. In the third example the main clause 'he said' is sandwiched between the two coordinated reported clauses. This makes it feel more immediate and more like direct speech. It is as if Eveline has stored away and internalised Frank's words.
2. Direct speech brings the characters to life. It creates a more direct connection between the characters and the reader. In a way the narrator usually stands in the way of this, whereas the absence of indirect speech allows the readers to observe the characters more intimately and work out the characterisation for themselves. Until the very end of the narrative, Frank's words are 'heard' only via Eveline's internalisation of them. It is therefore significant that Joyce chooses to allow Frank's own words to break through at the very end.

Task C

1. The subject complement clauses are underlined below:

   i. *She looked round the room, <u>reviewing all its familiar objects which she had dusted once a week for so many years</u>, <u>wondering where on earth all the dust came from</u>.*

ii. Then she had to rush out as quickly as she could and do her marketing, <u>holding her black leather purse tightly in her hand as she elbowed her way through the crowds</u> and <u>returning home late under her load of provisions</u>.
iii. Her time was running out but she continued to sit by the window, <u>leaning her head against the window curtain</u>, <u>inhaling the odour of dusty cretonne</u>.
iv. She would be on the sea with Frank, <u>steaming towards Buenos Ayres</u>.

2. The object complement clauses are underlined below; the relevant object noun phrase is in **bold**:

   i. She remembered **her father** <u>putting on her mother's bonnet to make the children laugh</u>.
   ii. Down far in the avenue she could hear **a street organ** <u>playing</u>.
   iii. She remembered **her father** <u>strutting back into the sickroom saying</u>: "Damned Italians! coming over here!"
   iv. She heard again **her mother's voice** <u>saying constantly with foolish insistence</u>.
   v. She caught a glimpse of the black mass of **the boat**, <u>lying in beside the quay wall</u>.

Task D

1. In example i the infinitive of purpose functions as complement of *the trouble was*. In ii the infinitive acts as a second complement clause, modifying the first (*putting on her mother's bonnet*). In iii. and iv. the infinitives postmodify the object noun phrases of the main clause (*God* and *her* respectively).
2. This is partly a matter of authorial style. Adverbials of purpose offer a more economical solution than subordinate structures and Joyce uses both to add further detail about people and objects that are important to Eveline. There is also a sense in which Eveline views both objects and people in terms of the functions they can afford her.

Task E

1. The copular verb phrases are underlined below:

   Her mother <u>was dead</u>
   That <u>was a long time ago</u>
   Everything changes
   She and her brothers and sisters <u>were all grown up</u>
   He <u>had been a school friend of her father</u>
   She had nobody to protect her
   Frank <u>was very kind, manly, open-hearted</u>
   She <u>felt elated</u>

2. Attenuation is achieved through lengthened verb phrases either with the addition of 'seem to', a modal verb (would) or an adverb (sometimes, always). Through

this Joyce adds doubt and speculation; it also physically distances the subjects from their complements, thereby achieving a similar effect visually.

Task F

1-2. Ellipsis is shown in brackets below:

> *She would not be treated as her mother had been [treated].*
> *Harry always sent up what he could [send].*
> *Her promise to keep the home together as long as she could [keep the home together].*
> *What would they say of her in the Stores when they found out she had run away with a fellow? [They would] Say she was a fool perhaps…*

3. Ellipsis is used to avoid the repetition of a word or phrase and therefore to keep the writing concise. It also supports the quality of colloquialisation of Eveline's thoughts.

Task G

1. *It* is a dummy subject in the following:

> *it was hard work*
> *it seemed a few weeks ago*
> *it was impossible*

In the third example the pronoun *it* refers back to the street organ.

2. Pronouns help avoid repetition of proper names or words mentioned previously in the sentence. The pronouns also emphasise the continuity of Eveline's thoughts and their use further suggests strong links in Eveline's mind between the 'he' who is her father and the 'he' who is Frank.

Exploring & Writing

Task A

1. i. Weeping, she saw him. = she was weeping
She saw him weeping. = he was weeping
ii. Weeping, she touched him. = she was weeping
She touched him weeping. = she was weeping
iii. Shivering with fear, she found him. = she was shivering with fear
She found him shivering with fear. = he was shivering with fear
iv. Snoring, she heard him. = she was snoring
She heard him snoring. = he was snoring
v. Realising the truth she killed him. = she realised the truth
She killed him realising the truth. = she realised the truth

2. Semantically, some non-finite complement clauses can only function as object complements. 'Snoring, she heard him.' doesn't make sense. 'Weeping, she saw him.' and 'Shivering with fear, she found him.' are also odd.

3. i. Weeping, she saw him. = subject complement clause
She saw him weeping. = object complement clause
ii. Weeping, she touched him. = subject complement clause
She touched him weeping. = subject complement clause
iii. Shivering with fear, she found him. = subject complement clause
She found him shivering with fear. = object complement clause
iv. Snoring, she heard him. = subject complement clause
She heard him snoring. = object complement clause
v. Realising the truth she killed him. = subject complement clause
She killed him realising the truth. = subject complement clause

4. A fronted complement clause always refers to the subject. When it follows the clause you have to use meaning clues to know whether it refers to the subject or the object.

Task B

1. i. Expecting a reply to her message, the computer was always on. This a clumsy as the non-finite clause doesn't directly refer to either the subject of the main clause.
ii. Sally, no emails arriving in her inbox, waited in vain. Here there is grammatical sense, but the ordering of the elements is odd.
iii. Pacing around the room in circles, she restarted the computer. This is unlikely as the two actions can't be simultaneous!
iv. Feeling hopeless, she deleted the dating app. OK.

2. Non-finite clauses should be used with caution. If there is no explicit link with the main clauses, the text may appear to lack cohesion unless semantics and common sense can be employed.

3. i. Grammatically, this works, but it's awkward because the order of elements suggests 'being dull' complements the subject 'he', whereas the writer intends it to complement the object 'the party'.
ii. OK
iii. Grammatically, this works with 'pouring wine' as a complement of the subject 'he'. As in Biii above, though, it doesn't work semantically as the two actions can't be simultaneous!

Task C

1. With ellipsis:

> Sally felt that if she had not heard of the app and decided to install it, she would never have put all her hopes on it and been so unhappy.

Suggested Answers

2. The sentence *'Sally would never have imagined she could fall in love, but then she did.'* is ambiguous. What is 'she did' referring to? falling in love or imagining it?

Task D

This is an exercise on reported speech. Speaker A begins the story thus: 'So we are driving along and this dog appears from the fields and there it is right in front of us. Alex panics and brakes the car suddenly, thank God, there aren't any cars behind.'

Speaker B reports the story, possibly saying: 'As they were driving along, a dog appeared from the fields and jumped right in front of the car. Alex panicked and braked the car suddenly but fortunately there weren't any cars behind.'

In reported speech, verb tenses change, and the simple or compound clauses may alternate with complex ones. Obviously, pronouns change too, and depending on who this is reported to, references to people or places may need additional explanation.

Task E

These are the initial three sentences:
I was sitting on this beach and it was quiet. I heard children screaming but I couldn't see them. I take a lifebuoy and run straight into the sea.

With the additions given in the instructions:
She was sitting on a beach; it was quiet and she appeared to be alone. She heard children screaming: 'Toooom, stay with us! Grab here! Heeelp!' She couldn't see the children and shouted back to where they were. She took a lifebuoy lying on a deserted boat and she ran straight into the sea to save the children.

Changes:
Attenuation: she appeared to be alone
Addition of direct speech: 'Toooom, stay with us! Grab here! Heeelp!'
Addition of reported speech: shouted back where they were
Addition of a complement clause, non-finite: lying on a deserted boat
Addition of an adverbial of purpose: to save the children

Review & Reflection

Task A

The main devices are complement clauses, finite and non-finite; reported clauses; adverbials of purpose; attenuation; ellipsis; dummy subjects.

Task B

Non-finite '-ing' clauses can be ambiguous if they can be interpreted as both subject and object complements. Make sure what is referred to and how, and let the reader make the right inferences from the meaning of the words. You also need to ensure events are simultaneous, or that you indicate completion of one before the other e.g. having poured the wine, he left the party.

Task C

Being distinct constituents, complement clauses, whether finite or non-finite, can be added nearly anywhere in the sentence to add further detail about the subject, object, or verb. Certain complement clauses can in theory be added infinitely, embedded into existing clauses. (This is the cat that killed the rat that ate the malt that lay in the house that Jack built…. etc!)

Attenuation can delay, ellipsis condense, and dummy subjects turn the focus away from objects and characters.

Chapter 10

Framing and Compiling: Sentences & the Text

Textual Analysis of the Narrative

Task A

1. Most of the sentences in the narrative are compound / complex.
2. Varying sentences constructions changes the pace and the rhythm of the piece. It also facilitates meaning, e.g. long, detailed constructions are rendered in compound/complex sentences, but matter-of-fact statements and important revelations are rendered in simple sentences. A pattern here is formed by simple sentences punctuating a succession of compound and complex sentences.
3. Most of the sentences in the narrative are declarative.
4. Varying sentence moods signal a shift in narration: interrogatives, imperatives and exclamative statements (appearing as minor sentences) are in direct speech which interrupts the third person narration.

Task B

1. *The two young children who had been left to her charge = The too young children that they had left to her charge*
   The organ player had been ordered to go away and given sixpence = They had ordered the organ player to go away and given him sixpence

Suggested Answers 165

Their passage had been booked = They had booked the passage
He was shouted at to go on = They shouted at him to go on

2. The changes draw the attention away from the subjects and what happened to them, and on to an unnamed agent who performed the action signalled by the verb.
3. This is a story that centres around Eveline and the people closest to her. These characters and any objects related to them are named and are used as themes of sentences. Interrupting this pattern with an impersonal 'they' diminishes the suffering of those involved as they are moved from the subject to the object position.

Task C

1. i. *Home!* is a minor sentence.
ii. is also a minor sentence as the main verb *say* lacks a subject. (The subject 'they' is implied but not stated.)

2. Minor sentences are exclamative; like direct speech, they interrupt the narrative as if readers needed to hear the characters talk or think aloud. They also introduce a colloquial feeling in the voice of the narrator.

Task D

1. The discourse markers are underlined below:

   Of course she had to work hard
   Of course, her father had found out about the affair
   In her home anyway she had shelter and food
   Her father was not so bad then; and besides, her mother was alive
   He would give her life, perhaps love, too

2. The discourse markers portray the voice of an empathetic narrator, who is in close proximity to the main character; the reader is thus encouraged to feel this way too.

Task E

1. The semi-colons signal a break in reading. We get to stop, then proceed to take in what follows, which might be an explanation or a contradiction.
2. Further uses of the semi-colon:

The man out of the last house passed on his way home; she heard his footsteps clacking along the concrete pavement
Her father used often to hunt them in out of the field with his blackthorn stick; but usually little Keogh used to keep nix

The effects are similar.

3. The dash introduces a further qualification about something just mentioned; it has therefore an explanatory effect.
4. Further uses of the dash:

   > *Then she would be married—she, Eveline.*
   > *It was hard work—a hard life—but now that she was about to leave it she did not find it a wholly undesirable life.*

   In these examples the dash also adds emphasis to what has just been said.

5. The narrative has 12 paragraphs (excluding dialogue):
    i. Setting
    ii. From the window / Childhood
    iii. The room / Present
    iv. Decision / Work
    v. The father
    vi. Frank
    vii. The father
    viii. Father and mother
    ix. Mother
    x. Frank
    xi. At the station
    xii. Indecision

Task F

1. Other examples of the lexical set of body parts:

   > *Her <u>head</u> was leaned against the window curtains and in her <u>nostrils</u> was the odour of dusty cretonne.*
   > *He was standing at the gate, his peaked cap pushed back on his <u>head</u> and his <u>hair</u> tumbled forward over a <u>face</u> of bronze.*
   > *She felt her <u>cheek</u> pale and cold*
   > *Her distress awoke a nausea in her <u>body</u> and she kept moving her <u>lips</u> in silent fervent prayer.*
   > *A bell clanged upon her <u>heart.</u>*
   > *All the seas of the world tumbled about her <u>heart</u>.*
   > *She set her white <u>face</u> to him*
   > *Her <u>eyes</u> gave him no sign of love or farewell or recognition.*

Through these words we get a close-up on the characters, so it's about proximity and intimacy between the reader and the characters in the story. Most of the set refer to Eveline and, again, they make the reader's relationship with her more intimate. The lexical set of body parts also stands in contrast to lexis relating to physical spaces, furniture and other objects.

Suggested Answers 167

2. Noun phrases: *all her life, a hard life, a wholly undesirable life, another life with Frank, her mother's life, that life of commonplace sacrifices, life*

   We notice the contrast between reality and a possible future with Frank.

3. Other examples of the lexical set of man-made spaces:

   close dark room, the sheds, the quay wall, portholes

   These and others add to the sense of Eveline being confined, trapped even, in her past and present.

4. Examples of the lexical set of sounds:

   footsteps, music, a street organ playing, her mother's voice, long mournful whistle, a bell, a cry

   The narrative is full of visual imagery; these words function as a sort of auditory imagery: readers can not only see the characters and the scenes but hear them too. There is a sense in which the auditory images are foreboding to Eveline.

5. Reoccurring images make the text cohesive, functioning as explicit links between different parts of the narrative. Semantically, they bring the story to life for the reader and act as points of reflection for readers to note and ponder the significance of the images

Task G

1-2. *Eveline heard his footsteps* (stative)
   The father used to hunt them in out of the field (dynamic)
   Eveline had consented to go away (stative)
   Eveline had never found out the name of the priest (stative)
   Eveline had hard work to keep the house together (stative)
   Frank took her to see the Bohemian Girl (dynamic)
   Frank used to call her Poppens (dynamic)
   Frank had sailed through the Straits of Magellan (dynamic)
   The father had read her out a ghost story and made toast for her at the fire (dynamic)
   Eveline wanted to live (stative)
   Eveline stood among the swaying crowd (stative)
   Eveline caught a glimpse (stative)
   Frank rushed beyond the barrier (dynamic)
   Frank still called to her (dynamic)

3. Joyce attributes stative verbs to Eveline and dynamic verbs to the father and Frank.
4. Eveline is facing one of the hardest decisions she would have to make in her life, and so most of her 'actions' take place in her mind whilst, physically, she is unable to act. On the contrary, both her father and Frank have a great effect on her, and this is illustrated through the active verbs related to their behaviour.

Task H

1. The sentences are of equal length and they are all long. The length is achieved through coordination, complement clauses and adverbials. The past perfect is also used in all of them. The repetition creates balance in the prose and, semantically, it shows that Eveline's thoughts about events in the past contain lot of detail, and that she can sustain her thinking for some time. It is also noticeable that Eveline's knowledge of Franks' former life depends only on what he has told her. She does not evaluate his activities as she has no information to judge them by: she (via the narrator) simply reports them.
2. All the sentences seem parallel in that they all include attenuation via the semi-modal 'used to'. This can be seen as indicating that Eveline, in some respects, views Frank as a father substitute. Although she has only met Frank relatively recently, it is significant she uses a form normally used to signify repeated actions to characterise and potentially, thereby, strengthen their relationship.
3. Modals, semi-modals and marginal modals such as 'would', 'consented to', 'was going to', 'about to', 'begun to' are used to distance the subject (Eveline) from the main verb (her actions). Attenuation is also achieved through parenthesis (look for phrases between dashes), rhetorical questions, minor sentences and exclamatives. All of these combine, by the end of the narrative, to make the final non-action inevitable.

Exploring & Writing

Task A

In general, Joyce seems to favour certain discourse markers and connectors, the use of dashes, minor sentences and occasional dialogue that may include interrogatives; parallelisms are found throughout the text, as is passive voice. Many of these features are memorable: deviant sentences beginning with 'but', the questions and exclamatives amidst otherwise relatively long sentences, the dashes which aren't all that common in other texts.

Below we re-write the final paragraph from the perspective of Frank:

> *Eveline! Evvy! I rushed beyond the barrier. Follow me! They shouted at me to go on but I still called to her. Come with me! And then she, Eveline, set her white face to me, passive, like a helpless animal. Her eyes gave me no sign of love or farewell or recognition — her eyes, hers, Eveline's.*

The passive voice wouldn't work as Frank is now in the subject position. We added an imperative, dashes, and noun phrases in apposition, which have the same effect.

Suggested Answers

Task B

Let's imagine a story with the theme of first kiss. There's a boy, Jack, and a girl, Jess, and another student, Toby, who is Jack's best friend. The setting is the school ball. Jack and Toby are chatting away when Jack realises he is bored and he'd rather be dancing with Jess. He had fallen for her a little while back.
Lexical sets to be used here include physical appearance, music, dance, drink.
Jess has always been a pretty girl but at the ball she is absolutely stunning.
Jack is distracted, feeling totally mad in love with Jess.
Toby isn't interested in love; he went to this ball just to get drunk and have a laugh.

Task C

This task is not easy: you could mimic somebody's style by copying their preferred sentence lengths and types, discourse markers, punctuation, any favoured parallelisms, but that's as far as you can go. To use somebody's else's vocabulary and somebody else's structural features in combination may not even be possible, because usually grammar and vocabulary work together to a powerful effect.

Having said this, let's simply take a couple of sentences from Joyce, and replace the content with words and phrases from Dickens:

She sat at the window watching the fog invade the landscape. Fog was everywhere. She could see it up the river flowing among green aits and meadows — and down the river rolling defiled among the tiers of shipping and the waterside pollutions of a great (and dirty) city.

You might agree that the poetic style of Dickens has almost disappeared, and his words somehow don't sit rightly with Joyce's structures.

Review & Reflection

Task A

A declarative sentence is a statement.
A minor sentence is formed of an incomplete clause, for example it might lack a subject or a verb
A lexical set is a group of words linked by a common theme.
A stative verb denotes a state of affairs or internal action, i.e. thought.
A dynamic verb denotes a physical, external action.
Passive voice shows what happens to the subject.
Parallelism is repetition of similar words and phrases.

Task B

Declarative sentence = *(There's) (f)og up the river, where it flows among green aits and meadows...* (As it's used it's an elliptical declarative sentence.)

Minor sentence = *Fog everywhere.* (Strictly speaking, this is an elliptical sentence, but could also be described as minor.)
Lexical set = *river, aits, meadows, marshes, heights*
Stative verb = none
Dynamic verb = *flows*
Passive voice = *defiled* (passive participle; there aren't any main clauses in the passage.)
Parallelism = *Fog up the river, where it... Fog down the river, where it...* In fact the whole paragraph relies on parallelisms.

Task C

From the features we have examined in this chapter, contrasting discourse markers, parallelisms that function as attenuation, minor sentences that bring Eveline's internal world to life, a great concentration of stative verbs in the main sentences, and the dense, intense even, descriptions of images that only exist in Eveline's head, all contribute to the sense Eveline is in turmoil and that her (lack of) decision is already inevitable.

Chapter 11

Bringing it all Together 1: A Holistic Review of Chapters 2, 3, 4, 5, 6, 7, 8, 9 and 10 Based on Narrative 1

Textual Analysis of the Narrative

Task A

1. The initial introduction of the protagonist as *she* both creates suspense (Who is 'she'?) and diminishes the character as if others (including the narrator) do not think it important to use her name. The pronoun *she* also functions as an explicit link between different parts of the narrative avoiding repetition of the proper name. Her name isn't introduced until several paragraphs into the story. It is significant, therefore, that Frank calls out her name at the end of the narrative.
2. Her father is never named; he is always 'the father'. Frank is named, as you would expect about Eveline's lover in a passage that packs a lot of information about him. 'He' is used most frequently, as a substitute for both 'the father' and Frank. This may suggest that Eveline tries to see in Frank the father figure she is lacking.
3. The structure simultaneously delays a revelation but also indicates Frank's significance to Eveline. Frank is significant to the reader because of Eveline.
4. In the next sentence Frank becomes the centre of our attention.

Suggested Answers

5. It is a powerful statement and it epitomizes how Eveline views Frank as her saviour.
6. The male and female pronouns are repeated a lot in a short amount of space. This way we get to follow each movement of these two people, at a moment of tension where everything is happening very fast and their fortunes are intertwined.
7. Other proper names are only mentioned once. They are less central in the narrative, but naming them precisely shows how Eveline has navigated her existence around the storing of small details
8. The first use of nouns in apposition emphasises Eveline's sense of wonder at what has happened to her; the second is probably just the name used to identify the child; in the final example the diminutive *Evvy!* (used for the first time) perhaps suggests Frank's sincerity and the depth of the relationship which simultaneously become apparent to Eveline and the reader.

Task B

1. 'Now' is Eveline sitting by the window in the first scene, and at embarkation point in the second scene.

2. Eveline sits in the window = 6
Eveline meets Frank = 5
Eveline plays in a field with children = 1
Eveline's mother dies = 2
Eveline does not leave with Frank = 7
Eveline brings up her brothers = 3
Ernest dies = 4

3. It's OK if you disagree, but you'll need to distinguish between the actual chronological order from the characters' point of view, and the arrangement of events in the narrative, which is about the order in which the narrator chooses to reveal different aspects of his characters' lives. These different 'times' often don't coincide in fiction.

4. *Her head was leaned against the window curtains* = simple past, passive voice, declarative
There used to be a field in which they used to play = simple past, declarative
Now she was going to go away like the others = past continuous, declarative
If she went, tomorrow she would be on the sea with Frank = conditional (simple past + modal)
He told her the names of the ships he had been on = simple past + past perfect, declarative

The first example introduces Eveline as a character with little agency, hence the use of the passive form. The next example highlights the way in which Eveline's present and future are shaped by her past. Example 3 distances Eveline from the 'going', and example 4 makes the action conditional upon Eveline's own choice and action. Example 5 indicates Eveline's knowledge of Frank's past is based only on what he has told her: it is a past of agency, energy and change, in contrast to her own.

Task C

1. Time adverbials of time are underlined below:

<u>One time</u> there used to be a field
And yet <u>during all those years</u> she had never found out the name of the priest
<u>Then</u> they had come to know each other
<u>One day</u> he had quarreled with Frank
<u>Now</u> she was going to go away

2. The adverbials above are fronted, in other words they are positioned at the beginning of the clause. They simultaneously set the time frame of what follows, but also delay revealing the action signified by the clause.
3. The adverbials of place are underlined below:

<u>In her home</u>, anyway, she had shelter and food
<u>Down far in the avenue</u>, she could hear a street organ playing
<u>Outside</u> she heard a melancholy air of Italy
<u>Through the wide doors of the sheds</u> she caught a glimpse of the black mass of the boat
<u>Amid the seas</u> she sent a cry of anguish

4. The adverbials above are also fronted (which is slightly more unusual), with similar effects: they simultaneously give a place reference for what follows hence emphasising the significance of place to Eveline, while also delaying the key message. In close proximity, they create parallelism, which creates rhythm and cohesion in the text.
5. Adverbials are used throughout the narrative, but not in the first and last few lines. The story ends the way it started, i.e. with the focus on Eveline, alone in the docks, just as when she was sat in the bedroom. Use of the simple past signifies the time frame. There is a visual symmetry created by these structures. Between these two scenes, we get to see other events and situations from Eveline's life, past and present, which feel at odds with each other: negative and positive aspects alternate, as if to mirror Eveline's confusion.

Task D

1. The repetition is a signal of time: the reader knows that the scene hasn't changed, i.e. that Eveline is still in the room reminiscing and contemplating the future. The word itself is used as a link between parts of the narrative that appear to be quite apart. Moving the function of the word from the object to the subject position, gives it agency, as if Eveline, who before was just watching the evening, has now succumbed to it.
2. *The window* is, for Eveline, the view of the world outside: she is in looking out, and this is significant. *The field* stands for her childhood and for fond memories of her playing with other children there. *Melbourne* is another faraway place,

Suggested Answers

suggesting that other people close to Eveline have migrated, as she is about to do herself. *Buenos Ayres* is where Frank chose to settle with her, but for Eveline is still a distant prospect. *The dock* is normally a place of departure, but for Eveline is a place of paralysis.

3. The objects are used symbolically—*the stick* for her father; *the black leather purse* for the money that was so hard to get and that she had to use very carefully; the *night-boat* for the darkness involved in migrating far away; *the iron-railing* that acted as a physical barrier between her and Frank; *the bell* for the turmoil she felt inside.
4. *She sat at the window watching the evening invade the avenue:* This is the beginning sentence; we know where she is sat and what time of day it is, the essential elements of the narrative that will unfold.

   Her father used often to hunt them in out of the field with his blackthorn stick: this is how Eveline remembers her father, hunting them with his stick; it might be trivial, but the detail is important for Eveline.
5. This is a long descriptive sentence which shows us what Eveline is looking at and the thoughts that preoccupy her. It gives the impression that Eveline is surrounded by objects, which she is reluctant to separate from, not realising that she is actually trapped by them and what they stand for.
6. The following sentences have a similar effect:

Then she had to rush out as quickly as she could and do her marketing, holding her black leather purse tightly in her hand as she elbowed her way through the crowds and returning home late under her load of provisions.
Through the wide doors of the sheds she caught a glimpse of the black mass of the boat, lying in beside the quay wall, with illumined portholes.

7. These sentences are short, mirroring the fact that Eveline is no longer looking at anything or thinking much; instead she stops moving, panicking at her inability to make a decision.
8. The discourse markers add emphasis, 'of course…', as if the facts following are natural or inevitable; both hard work and the controlling behaviour of her father restricted Eveline's sense of freedom. The *of course*s seem to introduce Eveline's voice into the narrative. It is she who is accepting of the inevitability.

Task E

1. *She looked round the room, reviewing all its familiar objects which she had dusted once a week for so many years, wondering where on earth all the dust came from.* = complex sentence with complement clauses
"He is in Melbourne now." = direct speech
She was about to explore another life with Frank. and *Now she was going to go away.* = both simple sentences
But she wanted to live. = a minor sentence

2. Stylistically, they link the two paragraphs. They also seem to be the narrator's intervention to add a short, factual statement about the setting and the scene. They contrast with the long sentences that describe Eveline's memory and thoughts that seem to linger.

3. *Escape!* = imperative or minor
She must escape! = exclamative, simple sentence
Frank would save her. = declarative, simple sentence

4. There are two interpretations. Without the quotation marks, they are integrated in the main narrative. So, the words belong to the narrator, who enlivens the prose by talking to his character. Another interpretation is that the words actually do come from Eveline, as if the narrator wanted to let us hear what the characters say or think, with only a slight intervention on his part. We are thus much closer to Eveline's thought, we know exactly what she says to herself. Technically speaking, this is free indirect speech or thought, something between direct and reported speech or thought.

5. The question is used in the same manner as the commands in 3 above.

6. "He is in Melbourne now." This is what Eveline remembers her father saying in relation to the photograph on the wall.
"Eveline! Evvy!" This is Frank's cry at the final scene.

In general, direct speech is actual words spoken by characters, either 'alive' in Eveline's memory or 'live' at the scene at the docks.

Task F

1. *Then she would be married—she, Eveline.* = 4
He said she used to squander the money = 5
Of course, she had to work hard, both in the house and at the business = 2
Was that wise? = 1
Frank would save her. = 7
But now she was about to leave it she did not find it a wholly undesirable life. = 6
Miss Gavan would be glad. = 3
She must escape! = 6

2. In general, Joyce does write from the point of an omniscient narrator. But he allows the reader to get closer to the characters, either through free indirect speech and thought as we saw in the previous task, or through features that express evaluation and attitude: the emphatic—*she, Eveline* and *Of Course;* the rhetorical question *Was that wise?;* the modality in *Frank would save her* and *Miss Gavan would be glad;* and the exclamative *She must escape!* There is thus a strong sense in which the reader 'hears' Eveline's voice throughout the narrative.

Suggested Answers

Exploring & Writing

Task A

Joyce's narrative is a tale of indecision and fear based around two scenes: the view from the window and the scene at the docks. From within these two scenes other characters are revealed, as well as objects and places, and details about these characters, objects and places. 'Time' seems to flow from the present to the past, and then to the future. How does the grammar used in the narrative achieve these effects?

Taking the narrative as a whole, let's consider the distribution, frequency and role of each grammatical structure.

Nouns and noun phrases are used frequently; **concrete nouns** outnumber **abstract** ones; and many are **heavily modified**. Why? There are details readers need to notice: the dusty window curtains, but also the dust on familiar objects in the room; the man of the last house passing by; the bright new houses they built, the field that once was there, before the houses, the play of her childhood in that field with other children. Every description, every **adjective** or **prepositional phrase**, tells us more and more: about her space at present, the world of her childhood, and people and incidents in between. The objects around her are oppressive and will eventually hold her back; her memories are vivid, intense even, as she can hear people's voices. More intense scenes are later revealed at the port. Just think about how the scene is described, the colours and the noises of the ships and the crowds, but also her internal world: 'all the seas of the world tumbled about her heart', as if the inside and the outside somehow merge into one.

Along with concrete and abstract nouns, we find **pronouns** and **proper names**, showing us which characters are linked to Eveline. Contrast, for example, how Eveline's father is referred to on several occasions: In the past: '*Her father was not so bad then...*'. In the meantime: '*When they were growing up he had never gone for her like he used to go for Harry and Ernest, because she was a girl; but latterly he had begun to threaten her and say what he would do to her only for her dead mother's sake.*' More recently: '*He said she used to squander the money, that she had no head, that he wasn't going to give her his hard-earned money to throw about the streets, and much more, for he was usually fairly bad on Saturday night.*' And finally: '*Her father was becoming old lately, she noticed; he would miss her.*'

Verbs and verb phrases capture everything that happens, had happened, might happen, in the past and the future. A few verbs are **stative** ('*she had consented*', '*she felt herself in danger*', '*she knew*') referring mostly to Eveline's internal world; the majority of the verbs are **dynamic**, again to match the frequency of concrete nouns and the intensity of her thought. A large number of verbs are **transitive**, describing actions with an impact on people or objects. Events and actions are described with detail (as in '*saying constantly with foolish insistence*'), not unlike the way people and objects are referred to via extended noun phrases.

Passives are used less frequently but are no less significant: '*He was shouted at to go on but he still called to her.*' This refers to Frank, who has no agency over his boarding of the ship; only over his calling to her.

Non-finite complement clauses, especially those formed by **participles**, add complexity to both the main actions and those involved in them. **Tenses** and **adverbials of time** point to different time frames. **Modal verbs** explore a possible future, Eveline married to Frank, what life in Argentina might look like, what people at home might think.

Looking at **clauses**, most reflect what one would expect from the combination of extended, modified noun phrases and varied verb phrases, in a mostly conventional order, S + V + x. Two things stand out though: (a) The **fronted adverbials**, e.g. *'Down far in the avenue she could hear a street organ playing.'*; *'Through the wide doors of the sheds she caught a glimpse of the black mass of the boat…'*; *'Amid the seas she sent a cry of anguish.'* These are important for two reasons, adding emphasis on the place, but also delaying the main verb, giving a sense of anticipation. (b) A few clauses where the subject is 'missing', in that the subject is no actual person or object, but an impersonal 'it', also called **'dummy subject'**, e.g. *'it would not be like that.'; 'It was hard work…'; 'It seemed a few weeks ago.'* These contrast with the majority of clauses that refer to people and objects involved in situations, as they express something that's above any character or thing, more objective and real.

There seems to be a rather heavy preference for **complement clauses**, both **finite** and **non-finite**. Finite complement clauses describe either nouns (*'all its familiar objects which she had dusted once a week for so many years'*) or verbs (*'wondering where the dust came from'*). Non-finite complement clauses are either complementing the subject (*'She sat at the window watching the evening…'*) or the object (*'She heard his footsteps clacking along the concrete pavement.'*)

Sentences express mostly **statements**, though there are a few **commands** (*'Come!'*) and **questions** (*'"Miss Hill, don't you see these ladies are waiting?"'*). The sentences are rather long, both **compound** (referring to a series of events) and **complex** (showing us events preceding, following, resulting from, etc. other events). **Embedding** results from frequent use of complement clauses (*'She has hard work to keep the house together and to see that the two young children who had been left to her charge went to school regularly and got their meals regularly.'*). Looking at sentences, it's worth noting the contribution of **punctuation**, the length of space between full stops, but also other marks, such as the dash, much favoured by Joyce. He uses that to illustrate something, to further qualify a noun phrase, as in the following: *'Then a man from Belfast bought the field and build houses in it—not like their little brown houses but bright big houses with shining roofs.'* The dash mark is another way to expand on a description.

Contrasts in **length** are noticeable. There are **minor sentences** (*'Home!'; 'Escape!'; 'No! No! No!'*), but it's the **simple** ones that have the most impact: *'Everything changes.'; 'He would save her.'* They emerge in a rather dense text like rays of hope disturbing the intensity and complexity of Eveline's thought. Joyce shows the character as both the producer and the product of the world which traps her, but also defines and supports her. Short, sharp phrases express hope but also fear, as Eveline is stifled with the overpowering sense of belonging to places, people, objects, which offer security but also devour her agency. All the participles and prepositional phrases reach through the story like tentacles!

Suggested Answers

The story is told in **third-person narrative**, but it's worth considering whose **viewpoint** is expressed at various points: *'Frank was very kind, manly, openhearted.'* Is this what Eveline thinks? Is this what everybody thinks?

For the most part, **direct speech**, unexpected and distractive, suggests vivid reminiscence and intense contemplation, interrupting Eveline's train of thought. In the last scene, at the port, the voices are more real, as is the inevitable end.

Review & Reflection

Level of analysis				
Word	Phrase	Clause	Sentence	Text
nouns	noun phrases	adverbials	passive voice	minor sentences
verbs	verb phrases	transitivity	complement	third-person
stative and dynamic verbs	prepositional phrases	passive voice	clauses	narrative
adjectives	adverbials	basic clauses	embedding	viewpoint
pronouns	transitivity	complement	'dummy subject'	direct speech
adverbs		clauses	simple sentences	
aspect		embedding	compound sentences	
tense		non-finite clauses	complex sentences	
modality		'dummy subject'	minor sentences	

Chapter 12

Bringing it all Together 2: A Holistic Appreciation of Narrative 1

Textual Analysis of the Narrative

Your own annotations should be a lot richer than the summary below which only covers key features.

Task A

1. The narrative is about a young woman who is weighing her decision to migrate with her lover. Eveline is the main character, then Frank and the father, and other characters that are brought into the story less directly, such as the woman at the Stores, as well as people from her past. Eveline is undecisive, the father is oppressive, Frank might be able to save her.
2. The voice of a third-person narrator is occasionally interrupted by direct speech. The point of view is that of the narrator, but there might be a few exceptions. There is a sense, at times, (as we have explored previously) in which the voice of

the omniscient narrator and Eveline's thoughts and voice merge e.g. *He was awfully fond of music; what would they say of her in the stores …?*
3. The main scenes are arranged in the order they take place: first inside the room, and the following day at the docks. Memories of events from the past disturb the linearity of the narrative. There is also, of course, a sense in which the end of the narrative is presaged from the beginning.

Task B

1. There are 12 paragraphs of varied length. Attention is drawn to discourse markers and transitions via direct speech. Quotation marks and dashes stand out.
2. The sentences are predominantly long, mostly compound/complex, and mostly declarative. Attention is drawn to simple and minor sentences, as well as to the parallel structures of long sentences with fronted adverbials.
3. There are plenty of complement clauses, especially non-finite ones, modifying both verbs and nouns. There are plenty of examples where the main verb is attenuated, or appears late in the sentence, following subordinate and complement clauses or adverbials.
4. There's a balance between noun and verb phrases, heavy noun modification, and a high proportion of verbs with adjuncts.
5. The lexis is general, formal, descriptive, and mostly Anglo-Saxon. There are some proper names, the nouns are mainly concrete, and there are plenty of adverbs. There are lexical sets corresponding to the room and the port. The verb tenses are mainly in the past but with occasional present tenses. There's transitivity, and modality on many of the verbs, and there are some copular verbs. Pronouns are used and interjections stand out.

Task C

1. As you look at your highlighted text, pay attention not only to features of high frequency, but also to those that are so infrequent they stand out.
2. Again, in summary: the adverbials and complement clauses achieve not just detail, but also transitions between thoughts, and contradictions between the present and a future life. Memories and events in the past are dense, matched by complex sentences. Simple sentences are timeless, and the present is loaded with intensity and sentence variation. The characters are given depth through details expressed by heavy modification and non-finite clauses. Proper names belong to people central in Eveline's life and memories. People in full control of Eveline's life are in the subject position of dynamic, transitive verbs; Eveline is in the object position, at the mercy of the father and her lover. Modal verbs amplify the uncertainty of the future. Suspended action is achieved through fronted subordinate clauses and adverbials. Direct speech and free indirect thought bring us closer to the characters, occasionally accessing their points of view directly. But

for most of the story the narrator manipulates the audience setting an objective point of view. Joyce's style is obviously unique to him, but in this story, we get a sense that his choice of grammatical structures and lexis work in combination to achieve a flowing and engaging prose, with enough detail to be able, as readers, to follow Eveline's glance out of the window and stand beside her at the docks the next day. A sense of paralysis is felt through strong imagery which in turn creates empathy on the reader's part.

Exploring & Writing

Task A

Hemingway's *Hills Like White Elephants* is similar in its theme. Also in third-person narration, it has more extensive stretches of dialogue, which is naturally in simpler language. Ellipsis and minor sentences stand out. We notice the parallel structures that describe the physical environment. A lot of detail is given not just to the setting, but also to secondary characters and their actions. There are fronted adverbials and noun modification, describing the landscape, but a preference for copular verbs makes for shorter, simpler sentences and heightens the sense of stasis and indecision. The exchanges between the two main characters are very intense at the beginning, until the girl asks the man to stop talking, unable to carry on herself, not unlike Eveline. The train station setting demands fast movement and action, and the verb phrases show exactly that. That this is another 'departure point' is hard to ignore too.

Review & Reflection

Task A

When you approach a text for the first time it's more natural to begin from the more general (narrative and aims) and narrow down to the more particular (lexis and lexical categories). This is what we called a 'top-down' approach at the beginning of this chapter. Once the analysis is complete, you can consider your findings in relation to the narrative and its aims, trying to make rich and meaningful connections between the grammatical structures and the narrative's meaning and effects.

A grammatical analysis uncovers textual features that would have gone unnoticed in a stylistic analysis that simply focuses on imagery and schemes and tropes. Having a good understanding of noun and verb phrases, for example, helps you uncover subtle features about the characters and the events respectively and, ultimately, provide a more in-depth analysis of the narrative and its crafting.

Chapter 13

Moving on 1: A Holistic Review of Chapters 2, 3, 4, 5, 6, 7, 8, 9 and 10 Based on Narrative 2

Textual Analysis

Task A (2 Morphemes, Words and Lexical Categories)

The feathery-white moon never let the sky grow dark; all night the <u>chestnut</u> blossoms were <u>white</u> in the <u>green</u>, and <u>dim</u> was the cow-parsley in the meadows.

1. chestnut = adjective, white = adjective, green = noun, dim = adjective
2. There are five adjectives in the sentence; (feathery-white, dark, chestnut, white, dim).
3. Colour used as noun (n) or adjective (a):

    i. *<u>grey-blue</u> clouds* = a
    ii. *eyelids <u>white</u> over eyes* = a
    iii. *For the glass held up an untrembling image—<u>white</u> and <u>gold</u>, <u>red</u> slippers, pale hair with <u>blue</u> stones in it* = all a
    iv. *the nocturnal <u>blackness</u>* = n
    v. *a <u>black</u> book* = a
    vi. *<u>pink</u> frocks out to dry* = a
    vii. *The cool <u>white</u> light* = a
    viii. *The cards were spread, falling with their <u>red</u> and <u>yellow</u>, faces on the table* = both n
    ix. *the <u>golden</u> fruit at its summit* = a
    x. *all the windows open, one <u>fiery-bluish</u>* = n

4. The title words 'from the outside' call for descriptive detail, including colour. White and black are symbolic of light and darkness, and by extension of the contrasts that run through the story; contrasts of class, values, and character. The reader follows the various elements that separate Angela from the other girls. White stands for Angela's purity and chastity, while the other girls are between 'white and gold', or colourless; the 'golden' fruit is symbolic of the social success that Angela is dreaming of.

Task B (2 Morphemes, Words and Lexical Categories)

1. *featureless, flawless, fearless, limitless* are all derivatives from the noun that is used as a base. The bound suffix *less* means without.
2. *innumerable* (in + number + able), *untrembling* (un + tremble + ing), *unmoulded* (un + mould + ed), *irresponsible* (in + response + able).
3. Each of the items draws attention to its opposite i.e. the base from which is it formed. This means Woolf can, at the same time, for example, evoke both *fear*

Suggested Answers

and *fearless*. Also, as with the colour terms, these adjectives create detailed and intricate descriptions and emphasise the contrasts between Angela and the others.

Task C (2 Morphemes, Words and Lexical Categories)

1. Other words from the set: *scullery, dairy, nunnery*
2. Words referring to place can be split into those relating to the college and those relating to Angela's home; by extension we might say that some are typically working-class places, and some are upper class; some belong to the sort of life Angela's mother was living, some belong to the aspirations attributed to college life.

   It is also possible to divide the items into sets of indoor and outdoor spaces. In general, the outdoor spaces suggest freedom and are the spaces which Angela yearns for, while the indoor suggest conventionality and restriction.

Task D (3 Nouns and Noun Phrases)

1. A. *Williams* = 4
   Angela = 2
   Angela, her other name being Williams = 5
   She = 1
   Angela Williams = 3
2. The narrator plays with notions of anticipation, unfamiliarity and familiarity, and confusion. There is a growing sense in which Angela is restricted by her name as by her roles in life.
3. The head nouns are underlined below:

   this bubbling <u>laughter</u>, this irresponsible <u>laughter</u>: this <u>laughter</u> of mind and body floating away rules, hours, discipline
   this good <u>world</u>, this new <u>world</u>, this <u>world</u> at the end of the tunnel

4. Both structures involve three repetitions of the same head noun: the first two with premodification and the third with postmodification. The repetition creates a poetic effect with balanced, rhythmic patterns that are emphatic in their meaning.
5. *There, in <u>the garden</u>, if <u>she</u> needed <u>space to wander</u>, <u>she</u> might find <u>it</u> among <u>the trees</u>; and as none but <u>women's faces</u> could meet <u>her face</u>, she might unveil <u>it</u> blank, featureless, and gaze into <u>rooms</u> where at that hour, <u>blank, featureless, eyelids white over eyes</u>, <u>ringless hands extended upon sheets</u>, slept <u>innumerable women</u>.*

In the order they appear, the pronouns '*it*' refer to 'space' and 'face'.

The noun '*space*' is postmodified by a non-finite complement clause (an infinitive of purpose: '*to wander*'); '*rooms*' is postmodified by a complement clause ('*where at that hour... slept innumerable women.*')

The adjectives '*blank, featureless*' appear first as object complements ('*she might unveil it*') and then as premodifiers of the noun '*eyelids*'.

There are 13 noun phrases in the sentence (underlined).

The sentence would most typically have ended with the verb '*slept*'; '*women*' is the subject of the complement clause and the fact that it's delayed until the end creates a poetic, almost mystical, effect.

6. The head nouns are underlined below:

> a <u>place</u> of seclusion or discipline, where the bowl of milk stands cool and pure
> From all the <u>rooms</u> where women slept this vapour issued
> Elderly <u>women</u> slept, who would on waking immediately clasp the ivory rod of office
> the <u>garden</u>, where the mist lay

All the head nouns are postmodified by a complement clause introduced by the complementizer, *where*.

Task E (4 Verbs 1: Tense and Aspect)

1. Most of the verbs in the narrative are in the simple past.
2. The first two excerpts are in the present simple, the third combines the past perfect continuous and the past simple, and the fourth is in the past perfect. The tenses create distinctions between the present in the narrative, the habitual and the events preceding the narrative.
3. 'were' is part of the conditional clause (*as if.../ if...*); it indicates an imagined hypothesis.
4. Most of the verb forms in the narrative indicate declarative mood.
5. '*We're not eunuchs.*' is emphatic, negative, and it's not clear who 'we' refers to.

Task F (5 Verbs 2: Modality, Catenation, Multi-Word Verbs)

1. The modal verbs are underlined below:

    i. *she needed space to wander, she <u>might</u> find it among the trees* (possibility)
    ii. *none but women's faces <u>could</u> meet her face* (ability, likelihood)
    iii. *she <u>might</u> unveil it blank, featureless* (possibility)
    iv. *A double light one <u>might</u> figure in Angela's room* (possibility)
    v. *Only Angela Williams was at Newnham for the purpose of earning her living, and <u>could not</u> forget even in moments of impassioned adoration the cheques of her father at Swansea* (inability)
    vi. *she <u>would</u> willingly have slept* (willingness, likelihood)
    vii. *one <u>must</u> tunnel into its darkness. One <u>must</u> hang it with jewels.* (obligation)
    viii. *the bushes <u>would</u> bow themselves* (likelihood)
    ix. *Elderly women slept, who <u>would</u> on waking immediately clasp the ivory rod of office.* (likelihood)
    x. *how <u>could</u> she express it?* (ability)

Suggested Answers   183

   xi. *how <u>could</u> one then feel surprise if, lying in bed, she <u>could not</u> close her eyes?* (ability, likelihood and inability)
2. The same modals may express different meanings, as shown in the brackets above.
3. This is a highly introspective narrative, and a lot of the actions signified by the verb are filtered through the confusion, contemplation and anxiety of the main character.

Task G (6 Verb Phrases)

1. The copular verbs are underlined below:

   all night the chestnut blossoms <u>were</u> white in the green
   dim <u>was</u> the cow-parsley in the meadows
   But here and there a light still burned
   The blinds <u>were</u> up.
   A mist <u>was</u> on the garden
   The mist <u>was</u> cleft
   Such <u>was</u> her discovery.
   chair and chest of drawers <u>looked</u> stately

2. The second example (*dim <u>was</u> the cow-parsley in the meadows*) is in the order complement + copular verb + subject, which is the reverse of the typical word order in English. The effect is poetic.
3. Copulas enrich the descriptions of the narrator's surroundings. They also create a feeling of stasis: the protagonist observes her world rather than having agency over it.

Task H (6 Verb Phrases)

1. The non-finite complements are underlined below:

   A. *Williams came in <u>yawning</u>.* (subject)
   '*I saw her <u>slipping in by the back gate with that old hat on</u>* (object)
   Good Bertha, <u>leaning with her head against the chair</u>, sighed profoundly (subject)
   From all the rooms where women slept this vapour issued, <u>attaching itself to shrubs</u> (subject)
   '*Ah,' breathed Angela<u>, standing at the window in her night-gown</u>* (subject)
   Angela, positively unable to sit still, like one possessed of a wind lashed sea in her heart, roamed up and down the room (the witness of such a scene) <u>throwing her arms out to relieve this excitement</u> (subject)

2. The subject complement *sitting on the floor by the* window grammatically relates to the subjects *body* and *mind*, yet these are an unusual choice for the complement.

The complement more naturally relates, in a semantic sense, to the *She* of the next but one sentence.
3. *The cards were spread, falling with their red and yellow* (subject)
   lying in bed, she could not close her eyes? (subject)
4. Woolf enriches the descriptions of the characters and their actions. She also suggests both the protagonist's keen awareness and a world in which every action is nuanced.

Task I (7 Basic Clauses)

1. The clause structures of the excerpts are indicated below:

   A. *Williams came in yawning* = subject + verb + non-finite complement clause
   Sally was on the floor = subject + verb + prepositional phrase
   A primvoiced clock struck the hour = subject + verb + direct object
   The cool white light withered them = subject + verb + direct object
   one may read it = subject + verb + direct object
   soft laughter came from behind a door = subject + verb + prepositional phrase

2. The narrative has few examples of S V O clauses because there aren't many transitive verbs. This, in turn, again suggests the lack of agency the protagonist and other characters have over their world.

Task J (8 Sentences)

1. a. *At that very moment soft laughter came from behind a door.* = simple
b. *'Because it's utterly and intolerably damnable* = minor
c. *Then the laughter.* = minor
d. *all night the chestnut blossoms were white in the green, and dim was the cow-parsley in the meadows.* = compound
e. *The mist was cleft as if her voice parted it.* = complex
f. *There, in the garden, if she needed space to wander, she might find it among the trees; and as none but women's faces could meet her face, she might unveil it blank, featureless, and gaze into rooms where at that hour, blank, featureless, eyelids white over eyes, ringless hands extended upon sheets, slept innumerable women.* = compound/complex

2. *For the glass held up an untrembling image—white and gold, red slippers, pale hair with blue stones in it, and never a ripple or shadow to break the smooth kiss of Angela and her reflection in the glass, as if she were glad to be Angela.* = compound/complex
Strange indeed to have this visible proof of the rightness of things; this lily floating flawless upon Time's pool, fearless, as if this were sufficient—this reflection. = complex
Now if the clock were issuing his commands, they were disregarded. = complex
The mist was cleft as if her voice parted it. = complex

Suggested Answers   185

The cool white light withered them and starched them until it seemed as if the only purpose of all these names was to rise martially in order should there be a call on them to extinguish a fire, suppress an insurrection, or pass an examination. = compound/complex

The dependent clauses, in each case, add a qualification to the main clauses; this serves to distance the main clause. This is particularly the case when the dependent clause precedes the main clause.

3. Compound/complex sentences occur most often in the narrative. This is typical of Woolf's stream-of-consciousness narrative, where one thought or observation leads to another. The effects are simultaneously meditative but fast. They also highlight the complex nature of Angela's world.
4. The 'missing' elements are shown in brackets below:

   [It was] *Strange indeed to have this visible proof of the rightness of things; this lily floating flawless upon Time's pool, fearless, as if this were sufficient— this reflection.*
   Such too [was the] *the resemblance, what with tiles, corridors, and bedroom doors, to dairy or nunnery, a place of seclusion or discipline, where the bowl of milk stands cool and pure and there's a great washing of linen.*

Woolf chooses not to include the ellipted elements perhaps to add to the poetic effect of her narrative and to increase the sense of flow in her stream-of-consciousnesses technique, as in 3 above.

Task K (9 Clauses Revisited)

1. The adverbials are underlined below:

   But <u>here and there</u> a light still burned.
   Anyhow the moment was glad the bright picture hung <u>in the heart of night</u>, the shrine hollowed <u>in the nocturnal blackness.</u>
   the cheques of her father <u>at Swansea</u>; her mother washing <u>in the scullery</u>: pink frocks <u>out</u> to dry <u>on the line</u>
   <u>At that very moment</u> soft laughter came <u>from behind a door</u>.
   Night was shared <u>in secret</u>
   <u>Beneath her</u> it lay—all good; all lovable

2. Most of the adverbials refer to places, as we would naturally expect from a descriptive narrative entitled '*A woman's college from the outside*'. They highlight the significance of the three main environments depicted: the outside world, the college world and Angela's home world.
3. <u>*Neither to Tartary nor to Arabia*</u> *went the wind of the Cambridge courts* = the adverbial is in the beginning of the clause, the subject at the end.

   Only Angela Williams was at Newnham for the purpose of earning her living, and could not forget <u>even in moments of impassioned adoration</u> the cheques of her father at Swansea; her mother washing in the scullery: pink frocks out to dry *on the line; tokens that even the lily no longer floats flawless upon the pool, but has a name on a card like another.* = the adverbial follows the verb but precedes the object.

She had been talking, <u>while the others played</u>, to Alice Avery, about Bamborough Castle; the colour of the sands at evening; upon which Alice said she would write and settle the day, in August, and stooping, kissed her, at least touched her head with her hand, and Angela, positively unable to sit still, <u>like one possessed of a wind-lashed sea in her heart</u>, roamed up and down the room (the witness of such a scene) throwing her arms out to relieve this excitement, this astonishment at the incredible stooping of the miraculous tree with the golden fruit at its summit—hadn't it dropped into her arms? = the first adverbial also 'interrupts' the main clause, as does the subordinate clause in the second part of the sentence

With constructions like these Woolf 'delays' the action signified by the main clause, thus creating a sense of anticipation. They also add to the poetical, mystical nature of the narrative.

Task L (10 Sentences and the Text)

1. *'hadn't it dropped into her arms?'* refers to Angela; the question might have been asked by Angela of herself, in the manner of free indirect speech, a half-way between the third person narration and direct (first-person) speech.
'how could she express it?' is less clear; it could be Angela again, or the omniscient narrator constructing the narrative in a fluid, doubtful manner.
'Indeed, how could one then feel surprise if, lying in bed, she could not close her eyes?' could again be Angela or the narrator or a mixture of the two; in this way the narrator takes us even closer to the main character.
2. The underlined are all passive constructions.
3. The passives remove the agency from the people or objects they refer to.
4. The constructions begin either with a subordinator or a complementizer (*for, which, such*).
    This deviates from the typical English word order and enhances the narrator's free-flowing and speech-like, but also poetic, style.

Task M (10 Sentences and the Text)

1. Like the questions we looked at above, the discourse markers add a sense of directness to the narrative, bringing us close enough to the characters to 'hear' their thoughts.
2. Direct speech brings the characters to life and shows both familiarity and immediacy.

3. Dashes add a further description, qualification or explanation of the referent they follow. Phrases between two dashes are parenthetical; removing them won't alter the sense of the rest of the sentence. Again, they add to the stream-of-consciousness technique where one thought follows quickly on from another.

    The effects are similar throughout the narrative.

4. In the first excerpt *'she might'* and *'blank, featureless'* are used in parallel structures.

    In the second excerpt parallelisms are formed around *'lay'* and *'laughter'*.

Another example includes 'as if she were' and 'as if this were' in the second paragraph. See also D 3 and 4 above.

Parallelisms serve both to draw the reader's attention to points of similarly and to coherence of voice throughout the narrative.

5. Examples of white objects: moon, blossoms, eyelids, light, vapour. Whiteness and brightness contrast with night and darkness, thus matching the central themes of the story: Angela is different from the others; she is also torn between her dreams and the reality of life.

The mirror, the glass and the reflections are also symbolic of the introspective and meditative style of the narrative.

Review & Reflection

Task A

The long compound/complex sentences, fronted adverbials and complement clauses, minor sentences and untypical word order give the narrative a sense of fluid thought and fleeting observations, but also confusion and frustration. Though much of the description is of the narrator's surroundings, it's her internal world that the reader is invited to focus on.

Task B

We think Woolf's narrative does blur the boundary between prose and poetry thanks to the rich imagery, symbolism, use of parallelisms, unusual orderings of elements in clause and sentence structures, as well as its rhythm and meditative tone.

Chapter 14

Moving on 2: A Holistic Appreciation of Narrative 2

Textual Analysis of the Narrative

As we suggested in the previous overview, your annotations should be a lot richer than the summary below which only covers key features.

Task A

1. The narrative is focused on Angela, a student at a women's college, who finds it hard to reconcile her working-class background, her parents' expectations, her own dreams, and the realisation that college life isn't what she thought, and that it may do little to help her materialise her aspirations. Angela is the main character, with secondary characters other students in the dormitory. Through the story we observe the differences between Angela and the other women, not just in their background, but also in terms of values, attitudes and behaviour.
2. The voice of a third-person narrator is occasionally interrupted by direct speech. The point of view is that of the narrator, but there might be a few exceptions, as we get to sense Angela's confusion through what could be free indirect speech or thought.
3. The main scenes are arranged in the order they take place: at the college, first outdoors and then indoors. The narrative reads like a continuous meditation, with only one instance of an 'intruding image', that of Angela' mother back home.

Task B

1. There are 9 paragraphs of varied length. Attention is drawn to discourse markers and transitions via direct speech. A few questions and dashes stand out, as does the limited dialogue roughly in the middle.
2. The sentences are long, mostly compound/complex, and mostly declarative. Attention is drawn to the very few simple sentences, and more so to the minor sentences, the untypical word order, the fronted adverbials and complement clauses, as well the parallelisms created by repetition of words and similar grammatical structures.
3. There are many complement clauses, both finite and non-finite that modify both verbs and nouns. There are plenty of examples where the main verb is attenuated, or appears late in the sentence, following subordinate and complement clauses or adverbials.
4. Noun phrases seem to outnumber verb phrases, partly due to poetry-like repetitions. There is heavy noun modification, and most of the verbs have adjuncts.

Suggested Answers

5. The lexis is general, formal, descriptive, and mostly Anglo-Saxon, with some formal words and expressions referring to college life. There are a few proper nouns, and the common nouns are balanced between abstract and concrete; there are plenty of adjectives and adverbs. There are lexical sets corresponding to the college surroundings and the life the character left behind, that of her mother. The tenses are mainly in the past but with few present tenses. There's limited transitivity, and a moderate number of modal verbs; copular verbs appear in relatively high frequency. Pronouns are used not only to refer to characters mentioned previously, but also in anticipation: 'she' is mentioned three times before the name Angela is revealed. Interjections are few and stand out.

Task C

1. As you look at your highlighted text, pay attention not only to features of high frequency, but also to those that are so infrequent they stand out.
2. Again, in summary: the modified noun phrases, adverbials and complement clauses achieve not just detail, but also put emphasis on the contrast between Angela and the other girls, and by extension, class differences, clashes between dreams and aspirations and the reality, and the juxtaposition of chastity and sexuality. The main character is troubled, confused, the narrator's observations are dense, and both of these are matched by complex sentences. The sentences are long, through both compounding and subordination, and they seem to merge into one another, just as the narration becomes very fluid, true to the writer's stream-of-consciousness style of writing. Places, objects and characters are given depth through details expressed by heavy modification and complement clauses. Proper names are given special mention, described more like printed labels that actual people. Dynamic, transitive verbs are few; a lot of the time Angela seems unable to express herself clearly—she gasps, breathes and sighs instead. Modal verbs amplify the confusion and uncertainty Angela is experiencing. Suspended action is achieved through fronted subordinate and complement clauses and adverbials. Direct speech and free indirect thought bring us closer to the characters, occasionally giving their point of view directly. But for most of the story the narrator manipulates the audience setting an objective point of view. Woolf's style is obviously unique to her, but in this story, we get a sense that her choice of grammatical structures and lexis work in combination to achieve a flowing and engaging prose, with enough detail for us to be able, as readers, to have a bird's eye view over the college and into the dormitory. The narrative is built upon contrasts: white and black, light and dark, laughter and pain, fun and frustration and anger. The reader is left with the bitterness Angela would ultimately experience, as she suddenly wakes from her dream and sees her real destiny in the face of her mother: from *'this lily floating flawless upon Time's pool, fearless, as if this were sufficient—this reflection...'* to *'even the lily no longer floats flawless upon the pool, but has a name on a card like another'* and then *'she cried, as if in pain.'*

Exploring & Writing

Our suggestion here would be to start by reviewing a short narrative you have written. To begin with, answer the recommended analysis questions. Following that, consider any alternative structures that achieve the same meanings you originally intended. Then think of possible ways to make your prose more poetic, or more detailed and precise, or more economical. For example, could you modify some phrases or sentences to achieve parallel structures? Or could you add noun modification to add detail? Or could you reduce the number of sentences, e.g. by elongating some of the existing ones with adverbials and complement clauses?

The idea here is to be playful in sculpting your use of language. Writing and rewriting will help you improve the quality of your prose, develop an awareness of its underlying structures and consider how its structures work to achieve your aims.

Review & Reflection

Task A

1. Didion uses two metaphors to describe grammar, and both are very revealing of different truths surrounding the notion of grammar. She says that grammar is 'a piano she plays by ear', and this is true of native users' intuition about the structures of their own language. Even if they lack knowledge of the metalanguage, they still have a subconscious awareness of what might sound right or not. Didion also says that grammar is like arranging objects to be photographed, and that such an arrangement is dictated by the picture one has in their mind. This points to the more conscious choices a writer has to make as they arrange their words, as we suggested in the previous task.
2. How about a cooking metaphor? How many different dishes can you prepare with the same 10 ingredients? Imagine the 'ingredients' are your vocabulary, the different 'preparation methods' are the structures that hold the words together and the condiments are the features you can add to achieve effects. All of these are easily modified, to achieve a range of different 'dishes', in other words, different styles and effects.

Task B

Our students often tell us that their original perception of grammar was as a dry subject heavy on terminology. They say studying through literature makes the process of learning more meaningful, and the metalanguage easier to understand and remember. They also suggest that a focus on grammar brings literature alive for them and makes them appreciate more some literature they already like. We hope that is the case for you too.

Task C

1. Conscious awareness of grammatical possibilities is a feature of good writing. Most writers would agree that writing and re-writing go together, and each choice or amendment involves lexical as well as structural considerations; simply put, being aware of the options saves time and effort.
2. Good reading is very important; a good reader can 'see around corners' as they navigate a text, understanding the subtleties of plot and character, the underlying messages and any symbolism, as well as the originalities of style including grammatical structure.
3. We hope you will appreciate this level and method of grammar learning as you progress with your studies in linguistics and/or literature. We hope that the creative writers amongst you have gained knowledge about the craft of writing which is not typically covered in core writing classes. We also hope that you will maintain the self-interrogating approach we have adopted in our final chapter.

A Final Word

We end this book the way we started, asking ourselves questions about 'good writing', the affordances of the English language and the linguistic choices authors make, consciously or otherwise, to tell a story, develop their narrative, engage the reader. This book was never meant to be an exhaustive description of English grammar, but by now you should feel you have acquired essential knowledge on constituent structure analysis and its metalanguage. You have achieved this in a natural enough way, not only through 'real-life' examples, but through two actual, continuous, lovely pieces of prose, crafted by two of the most celebrated names in English literature. We hope you've enjoyed these narratives and given yourself opportunity to apply some of the tasks to other literary texts. If you find yourself unable to read or write fiction without involuntarily paying attention to phrases, sentences and structures, then we are delighted, and happy to claim responsibility! If you want to take your knowledge and reading further, take a look at our recommendations on the following pages. Enjoy the journey, whatever your direction!

Recommendations for Further Reading

Grammar

The following text is an accessible and comprehensive introduction to Standard English Grammar for undergraduate students with no prior background in linguistics. You'll find definitions of grammatical concepts with examples, tasks, and a helpful commentary on prescriptive rules and current usage.

Huddleston, Rodney D., and Pullum, Geoffrey K. *A Student's Introduction to English Grammar*. Cambridge: Cambridge University Press, 2005.

Students of linguistics are likely to be introduced to one or more theories of grammar. Below are our favourite introductions to Chomsky's Generative Grammar and Halliday's Functional Grammar respectively.

Carnie, Andrew. *Syntax: A Generative Introduction*. Third edition. Chichester: Wiley-Blackwell, 2013.
Thompson, Geoff. *Introducing Functional Grammar*. Third edition. Abingdon: Routledge, 2014.

Literary Style

The following three textbooks offer excellent practical introductions to the study of literary style, covering considerations of sound, structure and meaning and their effects across the major literary genres. They offer excellent sections on narrative, point of view, as well as presentation of speech, thought and dialogue.

Leech, Geoffrey N., and Short, Mick. *Style in Fiction: A Linguistic Introduction to English Fictional Prose*. Second Edition. Abingdon: Routledge, 2007.

© The Author(s), under exclusive license to Springer Nature Switzerland AG 2022
S. Lavender, S. Varella, *Grammar in Literature*,
https://doi.org/10.1007/978-3-030-98893-7

Short, Mick. *Exploring the Language of Poems, Plays and Prose*. Abingdon: Routledge, 2013.
Simpson, Paul. *Stylistics: A Resource Book for Students*. Second Edition. Abingdon: Routledge, 2014.

Creative Writing

Creative Writing students interested in short narratives and stories in particular will find the following textbook an excellent source of information about developing and improving technique in the genre.

Cox, Ailsa. *Writing Short Stories: A Routledge Writer's Guide*. Second Edition. Abingdon: Routledge, 2016.

Those looking for more general guides on the processes of creative writing as well as advice on developing practical skills in fiction writing will find the following two textbooks very useful.

Boulter, Amanda. *Writing Fiction: Creative and Critical Approaches*. Houndmills: Palgrave Macmillan, 2007.
Cowan, Andrew. *The Art of Writing Fiction*. Abingdon: Routledge, 2011.

Short Narratives and Stories

If you would like to read more short narratives, the first obvious starting point is the other 14 narratives in James Joyce's *Dubliners*, originally published by Grant Richards in 1914. The narratives, widely available online, centre on a series of characters native to Dublin. Joyce returns to some of the characters from these narratives in his later novel *Ulysses* (1922).

Woolf's *A Woman's College from the Outside* was first published in 1926 as part of *Atalanta's Garland* by Edinburgh University Women's Union. The volume also contains narrative work by Katherine Mansfield. Woolf later extends some of the ideas from her own narrative in her essay *A Room on One's Own* (1929).

Many other narratives and short stories from a similar period in the early twentieth century are now out of UK and other copyright. The easiest place to access them is via the Project Gutenberg website: https://www.thoughtco.com/free-short-stories-from-project-gutenberg-2990442.

Indecision is a common narrative theme. You can explore more narratives about indecision by searching 'stories about indecision'. You can also use the following website: https://medium.com/the-junction/to-decide-and-to-move-on-79d75328dbe2.

We also strongly advise you to consult one of the many excellent anthologies of short narratives and stories. To name but one, *The Oxford Book of Short Stories*, edited by V.S. Pritchett and published by Oxford University Press in 1981, has been core reading on many undergraduate courses since its publication. Here, works are selected on their merits by a single editor.

Finally, short narratives and stories on a range of themes, of course, remain a highly popular and readily accessible genre. A brief online search of short narratives and short stories will quickly show you many more recent prize-winners and recommendations.

Enjoy and please keep exploring!

Glossary[1]

active voice   a construction involving a **transitive verb** whose agent is the **subject** position; e.g. *Jack watered the plant*. (See **passive voice**.)

adjective   a word that typically expresses a permanent or temporary attribute and is thus used in relation to a **noun**; e.g. a *red* dress / the dress is *red*. It is identified by its position in a clause, i.e. as noun **premodification** or as a **complement**. (See **attributive** and **predicative** adjectives.)

adjunct   a word or phrase which modifies a verb; usually an **adverb** or **prepositional phrase**, it is an optional part of the **verb phrase**; e.g. I met my friend *at the cinema*.

adverb   a word that expresses time, manner, place or circumstance; normally used as a verb **adjunct**; e.g. We walked *slowly*.

adverbial clause   a type of **subordinate clause** that has the same function as an **adverb**; e.g. *Whenever we meet*, we talk for hours.

adverbial   a phrase that has the same function as an **adverb**; e.g. We talked *for hours*.

affirmative   a quality of the sentence, known as **mood**, that expresses a positive statement; e.g. *We like talking*. (See **declarative; negative**.)

affix   a **bound morpheme** attached to a **free morpheme** for the purpose of **derivation** or **inflection** e.g. *unimportant, talked*. (See **prefix; suffix**.)

apposition   a structure in which two **noun phrases** with identical referents are placed next to each other; e.g. *Prof. Phillips, my colleague*, retired.

aspect   a quality of the **verb** indicated by its form and which declares whether the action is continuing, or completed, etc. (See **continuous aspect; perfective aspect; simple aspect**).

---

[1] Please note: Terms in **bold** within a definition have separate entries; forms in *italics* illustrate the term in question.

attenuation a structure which lengthens the distance between the **subject** and its **complement** thus weakening the link between the two; e.g. She *seemed to be quite* confused.

attributive adjective an **adjective** within a **noun phrase**, i.e. one that modifies a noun; e.g. a *red* dress. (See **predicative adjective**.)

auxiliary verb any form of the verbs *be* or *have* whose single purpose is to form the **tense** or **aspect** of the **main verb**; e.g. I *have* studied linguistics. (See **modal verb**.)

basic clause a syntactic category that includes a **noun phrase** and a **verb phrase**, functioning as **subject** and **predicate** respectively.

bound morpheme a part of a word that is meaningless on its own and is used in word formation to derive new words or change the grammar of existing words; e.g. *un*-happy (See **free morpheme**; **derivation**; **inflection**.)

catenation a structure made up of two verb forms 'chained' together; e.g. I *was persuaded to go*.

clause a syntactic category larger than a **phrase** and smaller than a **sentence**. (See **main** and **subordinate** clause.)

closed class/ category a category of words that have mainly grammatical function, such as **determiners**, **pronouns** and **prepositions**; such a category is 'closed', in that it does not readily accept new members. (See **function word**.)

complement clause a **finite** or **non-finite clause** which modifies a noun (**noun-complement clause**), e.g. The new colleague *who started yesterday* is nice, or a verb (**verb-complement clause**), e.g. She said *that she liked her office*.

complement 1. part of the **verb phrase** other than the head verb, usually a **noun phrase** functioning as **direct** or **indirect object**. 2. a particular term for the word that follows a **copular verb** and which shares the same referent with the **subject** of the verb phrase (**subject complement**) or the **object** of the verb phrase (**object complement**).

complementizer a **function word** that marks a complement clause, e.g. *who* and *that*: The new colleague *who started yesterday* is nice. She said *that* she liked her office.

complex sentence a sentence made up of a **main** and a **subordinate clause**; e.g. *When he has free time, he plays tennis.*

compound sentence a sentence made up of two **main**, or **coordinate, clauses**; e.g. *He plays tennis but he prefers squash.*

compound/complex sentence a sentence that combines **coordinate** and **subordinate clauses**. *When he has free time he plays tennis but in the winter he plays squash.*

compounding a process of word formation in which two **free morphemes** are joined into a single word; e.g. *foot-ball*.

conjunction a grammatical word that joins similar structures; e.g. He plays tennis *and* squash; He plays tennis *but* he prefers squash. (See **coordinating conjunction** and **subordinating conjunction**.)

constituent a distinct syntactic unit within the overall structure of a sentence; e.g. the **noun phrase** *This grammar book* in the **sentence** *This grammar book is helpful.*

content word a word with semantic function and which belongs to the **open category** which is expandable; it can therefore be a **noun**, **adjective**, **verb** or **adverb**. (See **lexical word**.)

continuous aspect a quality of the **verb** indicated by its form which declares that the action signified by the verb is continuing; e.g. He *is playing* tennis. (See **progressive aspect**.)

coordinate clause one of two or more **main clauses** joined together in **coordination**.

coordinating conjunction also known as **coordinator**, it joins **noun phrases**, or **verb phrases**, or **clauses** in **coordination**; e.g. He met his friends *and* they played tennis.

coordination a structure that includes conjoined structures that are similar, as in a **compound sentence**; *He met his friends and they played tennis.*

coordinator another term for **coordinating conjunction**.

copular verb a verb that takes a **complement** (sense 2); e.g. Jack *is* a composer.

declarative a quality of the sentence, known as **mood**, that expresses a statement; e.g. *We like talking*. (See **indicative**.)

dependent clause another term for **subordinate clause**.

derivation a process of word formation in which the addition of a **bound morpheme** creates a new word, sometimes of a different **lexical category**, from an existing word; e.g. *talk > talk-ative.*

determiner a grammatical word that is usually part of noun phrase and modifies the head noun; e.g. *the* red dress.

direct object part of the **verb phrase**, often a **noun phrase** that follows a **transitive or ditransitive verb** and which expresses an object involved in the action expressed by the verb; e.g. He told her *the truth.*

direct statement words in a narrative as uttered by one of the characters, usually appearing in quotation marks. (See **reported clause/ statement**.)

discourse marker a word that functions as a connector, not strictly part of the grammatical structure of the clause, but loosely added to give flow to a text; e.g. *Besides*, he is good at tennis.

ditransitive verb a **verb** that takes a **direct** and **indirect object**; e.g. He *told* her the truth.

dummy subject a semantically empty word that functions as the **subject** in a clause; e.g. *It's* raining. *There* was a storm.

dynamic verb a **verb** that signifies action, which has an effect on somebody or something else. (See **stative verb**.)

ellipsis a **sentence** that lacks **words** or **phrases** that would have been expected to complete a structure; the meaning of these words or phrases is inferred by the rest of the sentence; e.g. Jack plays tennis but Jess doesn't *[play tennis]*.

embedding the inclusion of one **constituent** into another in a **clause** or **sentence**; e.g. the clause *(that) you recommended* is embedded in the larger clause *The grammar book you recommended is very helpful.*

exclamative a full or **minor sentence** that expresses an emotion; e.g. *Wonderful! Have a nice day!*

finite complement clause a **complement clause** which includes a **finite**; e.g. Jack, *who played every evening*, is good at tennis. (See **non-finite complement clause**.)

finite a **verb** marked for **tense**; e.g. He *played* every evening.

form the internal structure or position of a word or larger unit which, along with **function**, determines its **category**, whether **lexical** (for individual words) or **syntactic** (for larger units like **phrases** and **clauses**).

free morpheme a part of a word that constitutes a word in itself and is used in word formation to derive new words or change the grammar of existing words; e.g. un-*happy*; or in **compounding** to form a new word out of two; e.g. *foot-ball* (See **free morpheme**; **derivation**; **inflection**.)

function word a word with grammatical function which belongs to the **closed category** which is non-expandable; it can therefore be a **pronoun, preposition, conjunction and interjection**. (See **grammatical word**.)

function the grammatical purpose of a word or structure. Compare **form**.

grammar the system by which **words** and **morphemes** are organised into larger units, such as **phrases**, **clauses** and **sentences**; the description of such a system; a branch of **linguistics** concerned with **morphology** and **syntax**.

grammatical word another term for **function word**.

head noun the most central element in a **noun phrase**; the **noun** around which a noun phrase is formed.

head verb the most central element in a **verb phrase**; the **verb** around which a verb phrase is formed.

imperative a quality of the sentence, known as **mood**, that expresses a command; e.g. *Say something*!

independent clause another term for **main clause**.

indicative another term for **declarative**.

indirect object part of the **verb phrase**, often a **noun phrase** that follows a **ditransitive verb** and which expresses the beneficiary of the action expressed by the verb; e.g. He told *her* the truth.

infinitive a type of **non-finite** verb; sometimes preceded by *to*; e.g. He wants *to play* tennis.

inflection a process of word formation whereby the addition of a **bound morpheme** changes the grammatical form of an existing word; e.g. *cat-s*.

interjection a word or phrase that expresses an emotional reaction; words or **minor sentences** as in *Ouch!* or *Wow!* etc. form a category of their own.

interrogative a quality of the sentence, known as **mood**, that expresses a question; e.g. *Do you like talking*?

intransitive verb a **verb** that does not take an **object**, i.e. a verb that signifies action that doesn't involve anything or anybody else; e.g. He *works* hard.

lexical category Any one of the few different categories of words, which represent a way of organising lexical items according to their grammatical or semantic function, such as **noun**, **adjective**, **verb**, **adverb**, **pronoun**, **preposition**, **determiner**, **conjunction** and **interjection**. (See **word class**.)

lexical set a group of words linked by a common theme.

lexical word another term for **content word**.

linguistics the scientific study of language.

main clause an **independent clause** that can stand alone in a **complex sentence**; one part of a **compound sentence**.

main verb the part of the verb that contains lexical formation, i.e. excluding any **auxiliaries** or **modals**; e.g. she might *come*.

marginal modal any form of verbs such as *be going to* and *be about to* which works like an **auxiliary verb** in conjunction with the **main verb** and, like a **modal verb**, expresses **modality**, in this case future intention or immediate action respectively; e.g. She *is going to* go. She *was about to* leave. (See **semi-modal**.)

minor sentence a sentence not following the conventional **subject—verb—object** word order; often missing either the subject, e.g. *Will do!* or the verb, e.g. *No parking in front of the gate*; sometimes made up of just a single word, e.g. the exclamative *Morning!*

modal verb a particular category of verb that functions as an **auxiliary** and adds **modality** to the **main verb**; this is a small category and includes *can, could, shall, should, will, would, may, might, must,* and *ought*; e.g. She *might* study linguistics.

modality a quality of the verb, expressed through its form (**modal verb** + main verb), and which distinguishes it according to the degree of likelihood or necessity of the action signified by it; e.g. She *may come.* She *must come.*

mood a quality of a sentence indicated by the verb form that identifies it as a statement, command or question. (See **declarative**; **imperative**; **interrogative**.)

morpheme an identifiable part of a word, e.g. un-happy, cat-s. (see **free** and **bound morpheme**.)

morphology the study of word structure; part of the **grammar** of a language.

multi-word verb a verb made up of more than one word; e.g. She *put up with* him.

negative a quality of the sentence, known as **mood**, that expresses a negative statement; e.g. *We don't like talking*. (See **affirmative; declarative**.)

non-finite complement clause a **complement clause** which includes a **non-finite**; e.g. *Playing every evening*, Jack is good at tennis. (See **finite complement clause**.)

non-finite a **verb** not marked for **tense**; e.g. He played to *win*.

noun phrase a **phrase** formed around a **noun** and may also include a determiner, an adjective, or other forms of pre- and postmodification; e.g. *His tennis talent* is remarkable.

noun a **lexical category** which signifies a person, object, or **proper name**; e.g. He wants to be a *champion*.

noun-complement clause a **complement clause** which modifies a noun; e.g. The new colleague *who started yesterday* is nice.

object complement a **complement** (sense 2) of the **object** of a **clause**; e.g. Tennis makes him *happy*. (See **subject complement**.)

object part of the **verb phrase**, often a **noun phrase** that follows a **transitive or ditransitive verb** and which expresses an object involved in the action, or the beneficiary of the action, expressed by the verb; e.g. He told *her the truth*. (See **direct object**; **indirect object**.)

open class/ category a category of words that have mainly semantic function, such as **nouns, adjectives, verbs** and **adverbs**; such a category is 'open', in that it readily accepts new members. (See **content word**.)

paragraph a distinct section of a **text**, made up of one or more **sentences** and usually dealing with a single theme.

parallelism the repetition of similar structures; e.g. *I came, I saw, I conquered.*

part of speech another term for **lexical category.**

participle a type of non-finite verb; often ending in *-ing* or *-ed*; e.g. The tennis player *playing* tomorrow is good.

passive voice a construction involving a **transitive verb** whose agent is not in the **subject** position, but which may be included in a **prepositional phrase**; the subject is the person or thing benefiting or suffering from the action expressed by the verb; e.g. *The plant was watered by Jack.* (See **active voice**.)

past continuous a **tense** and **aspect** combination which signifies a continuous action in the past; e.g. He *was playing* tennis all day yesterday.

past perfect continuous a **tense** and **aspect** combination which signifies a continuous and completed action in the past; e.g. He *had been playing* tennis while studying but stopped when he got a job.

past perfect a **tense** and **aspect** combination which signifies a completed action in the past; e.g. He *had played* tennis before he joined a squash club.

past a **tense** which signifies that the action expressed by the **verb** took place in the past; e.g. He *played* tennis last week.

perfective aspect a quality of the **verb** indicated by its form (i.e. inclusion of has, have, had) and which declares that the action signified by the verb is completed; e.g. He *had* won tournaments before.

phrase a **syntactic category** based on a **lexical category**; e.g. **noun phrase, verb phrase, prepositional phrase.**

postmodification part of the **noun phrase**, a word or phrase that describes or specifies the **head noun**; it follows the head noun e.g. the **complement clause** in The old friend *who moved to the US*. (See **premodification**.)

predicate the second part of a **basic clause**, following the **subject;** it includes the **verb** and any word or phrase that depends on it; e.g. Jack *plays tennis*.

predicative adjective an **adjective** functioning as **complement** (sense 2); i.e. following a **copular verb**, i.e. one that modifies a noun; e.g. The dress is *red*. (See **attributive adjective**.)

prefix a **bound morpheme** attached in front of a **free morpheme** for the purpose of **derivation** or **inflection**; e.g. *un-happy*. (See **affix; suffix**.)

premodification part of the **noun phrase**, a word or phrase that describes or specifies the **head noun**; it precedes the head noun e.g. the **adjective** in The *old* friend who moved to the US. (See **postmodification**.)

preposition a **function word** which signifies location, direction, relation, etc. e.g. *on, in, to, above, below, with*.

prepositional phrase a **phrase** formed around a **preposition**; it's normally introduced by a preposition which is followed by a noun phrase; e.g. He plays tennis *with a friend*.

present continuous a **tense** and **aspect** combination which signifies a continuous action in the present; e.g. He *is playing* tennis now.

present perfect continuous a **tense** and **aspect** combination which signifies a continuous and completed action in the present; e.g. He *has been playing* tennis while studying.

present perfect a **tense** and **aspect** combination which signifies a completed action in the present; e.g. He *has played* tennis for years.

present a **tense** which signifies that the action expressed by the **verb** takes place in the present; e.g. He *plays* tennis.

progressive aspect another term for **continuous aspect**.

pronoun a **function word** which is used instead of a noun in a **noun phrase**; e.g. *he, she, they, who?* etc.

proper noun/ name a noun that refers to a person, place or other entity by name; e.g. *London* is the capital of the *UK*.

punctuation the use of special marks in a **text** to facilitate reading and understanding; e.g. the comma, full stop, dash, parenthesis, etc.

relative pronoun please see **complementizer**.

reported clause/ statement words in a narrative presumably uttered by one of the characters but reported by the narrator. (See **direct statement**.)

semi-modal the verbs *used to* or *have to* which are used like an **auxiliary verb** in conjunction with the **main verb** and, like a **modal verb**, express **modality**, in this case repetition of action or obligation respectively; e.g. She *used to* play tennis. She *had to* quit playing. (See **marginal modal**.)

sentence a **syntactic category** made up of one or more **clauses**.

simple aspect a quality of the **verb** indicated by its form and which declares that the action signified by the verb is neither continuous nor completed, but habitual.

simple past a **tense** and **aspect** combination which signifies a habitual action in the past; e.g. He *played* tennis.

simple present a **tense** and **aspect** combination which signifies a habitual action in the present; e.g. He *plays* tennis.

simple sentence a **sentence** made up of one (**main**) **clause**.

stative verb a **verb** that signifies a state of being rather than action, and which therefore has no effect on somebody or something else. (See **dynamic verb**.)

subject complement a **complement** (sense 2) of the **subject** of a **clause**; e.g. He is *happy*. (See **object complement**.)

subject   the first part of a **basic clause**, preceding the **predicate;** it signifies the person or thing involved in the action expressed by the **verb**; e.g. *Jack* plays tennis.

subordinate clause   a **dependent clause**, i.e. a clause that cannot stand on its own but depends on a **main clause** in a **complex sentence**.

subordinating conjunction   also known as **subordinator**, it introduces the **subordinate clause** in a **complex sentence**; e.g. He played tennis *before* he met his friends.

subordination   the addition of **subordinate clause** to a **main clause** to form a **complex sentence**; e.g. He played tennis *before he met his friends*.

subordinator   another term for **subordinating conjunction.**

suffix   a **bound morpheme** attached at the end of **free morpheme** for the purpose of **derivation** or **inflection**; e.g. *boy-hood*. (See **affix; prefix**.)

syntactic category   an identifiable structure with particular characteristics, such as a **phrase**, **clause** or **sentence**.

syntax   the study of sentence structure; part of the **grammar** of a language.

tense   a quality of the **verb** indicated by its form and which signifies whether the action takes place in the present or past or future.

text   a piece of writing often made up of different **paragraphs**.

transitive verb   a **verb** that takes a **direct object**, i.e. a verb signifying an action that involves somebody or something else; e.g. He *plays* tennis.

transitivity   in a **clause**, the relationship between **subject** and **predicate**, which is largely determined by the meaning of the **verb**.

verb phrase   a **phrase** formed around a **verb** and consisting of a **head verb** and its **complement**(s); e.g. He *plays tennis*.

verb   a **lexical category** which signifies an action or state of affairs; e.g. He *plays* tennis.

verb-complement clause   a **complement clause** which modifies a verb; e.g. She said *that she liked her office*.

word   a lexical item; a member of any of the **lexical categories,** with semantic or grammatical function.

word class   another term for **lexical category.**

Index

A

Active voice, 76
Adjective, 12, 14–17, 20, 22, 86, 90, 95, 103–105, 115, 124–129, 132, 134, 175, 180–182, 189
Adjunct, 41, 42, 49, 95, 115, 150, 178, 188
Adverb, 12, 15, 16, 33–35, 42–44, 47, 86, 124–128, 136, 150, 160, 178, 189
Adverbial, 42–44, 46–48, 58, 67, 70, 73, 87, 88, 90, 95, 96, 108, 109, 115, 116, 136, 146–150, 153, 159, 160, 163, 168, 172, 176, 178, 179, 185, 187–190
Adverbial clause, 58, 62
Affirmative, 29, 31, 75
Affix, 125
Apposition, 21, 87, 168, 171
Aspect, v, x, xi, xiv, 7, 27–32, 66, 67, 75, 86, 87, 90, 93–96, 105–106, 113–117, 124, 134–137, 139, 145, 149, 171, 172, 182
Attenuation, 65, 67, 160, 163, 164, 168, 170
Attributive adjective, 130
Auxiliary verb, 29, 124, 144

B

Basic clause, 51–56, 85, 90, 95, 107, 115, 151, 154, 184
Bound morpheme, 11, 12, 16, 125, 128

C

Catenation, 33–39, 106, 140–141, 143, 145, 182–183
Clause, xiii, xiv, 1–3, 33, 41, 43, 44, 46, 47, 51–62, 65–73, 76, 77, 80, 85–90, 95, 103, 107–110, 113, 115, 117, 120, 121, 128, 140, 148, 151–157, 159, 162–164, 169, 172, 176, 178, 182, 184–187
Closed category, 12, 128
Complement, 41–43, 45, 49, 53, 59, 67, 69–71, 95, 106, 107, 115, 146, 150, 151, 156, 161, 162, 183, 184
Complement clause, 21, 59, 60, 65–68, 73, 89, 90, 95, 115, 134, 156, 159, 160, 162–164, 168, 173, 176, 178, 181, 182, 187–190
Complementizer, 21, 59, 65, 66, 68, 107, 159, 182, 186
Complex sentence, 58–61, 63, 76, 85, 89, 90, 155–158, 164, 178, 189
Compound/complex sentence, 59, 62, 164, 185, 187
Compounding, 189
Compound sentence, 58, 60–62, 85, 86, 90, 155–157
Conjunction, 12, 58, 61, 76–77, 85, 95, 115, 128, 154, 155, 157
Constituent, 11, 27, 34, 41, 51, 164, 193
Content word, 12, 86, 125

Continuous aspect, 28, 29
Coordinate clause, 59, 158
Coordinating conjunction, 58, 155
Coordination, 58, 168
Coordinator, 58, 155
Copular verb, 43, 45, 48, 67, 70, 95, 106, 115, 147, 150, 160, 178, 179, 183, 189

D
Declarative, 29, 31, 75, 78, 83, 144, 164, 169, 171, 178, 182, 188
Dependent clause, 58, 65, 85, 185
Derivation, 12
Determiner, 12, 20, 95, 115, 128, 129
Direct object, 42, 53, 69, 147, 152
Direct statement, 66
Discourse marker, 76–77, 79, 110, 165, 168–170, 173, 178, 186, 188
Ditransitive verb, 42, 45, 46, 48, 76, 146, 150
Dummy subject, 65, 68, 71, 90, 161, 163, 164, 176
Dynamic verb, 78, 83, 90, 167, 169

E
Ellipsis, 59, 65, 67–68, 71, 72, 121, 161–164, 179
Embedding, 90, 176
Exclamative, 75–77, 164, 165, 168, 174

F
Finite, 67, 73, 95, 115, 163, 164, 176, 188
Finite complement clause, 176
Form, x, xi, xiv, xvi, 2, 12, 14, 19, 21, 28, 29, 31–34, 37, 52, 62, 65–67, 73, 75, 76, 78, 80, 82, 85, 86, 106, 124–126, 129, 135, 136, 144, 154, 155, 168, 171, 182, 187
Free morpheme, 11, 12, 15, 16, 125, 128
Function, 12–14, 16, 19, 20, 42, 59, 66, 67, 71, 103, 104, 123, 124, 128, 136, 145, 155, 160, 162, 167, 170, 172
Function word, 12

G
Grammar, v, ix–xiv, xvi, 1–5, 27, 73, 90, 93, 113, 117–122, 145, 150, 169, 175, 190, 191, 193
Grammatical word, 12

H
Head noun, 20–24, 52, 65, 105, 129–133, 181, 182
Head verb, 42

I
Imperative, 29, 31, 32, 68, 75–77, 89, 137, 138, 164, 168
Independent clause, 58, 155
Indicative, 29, 75
Indirect object, 42, 43, 53, 76, 147, 150, 152
Inflection, 12
Infinitive, 28, 66, 67, 70, 160, 181
Interjection, 12, 76, 178, 189
Interrogative, 29, 31, 32, 75, 109, 136–138, 141, 164, 168
Intransitive verb, 43, 146

L
Lexical category, 11–17, 19, 27, 30, 41, 86, 103–104, 123, 126, 179–181
Lexical set, 11, 77, 80, 82, 104, 111, 166, 167, 169, 178, 189
Lexical word, xiii, 12, 15
Linguistics, x, xiv, 1, 2, 4, 95, 115, 120, 191, 193, 195

M
Main clause, 58, 85, 86, 95, 108, 115, 159, 160, 162, 170, 185, 186
Main verb, 29, 32–34, 124, 139, 143, 165, 168, 176, 178, 188
Marginal modal, 34, 36, 37, 142, 168
Minor sentence, 76, 79, 83, 89, 90, 108, 164, 165, 168–170, 176, 178, 179, 187, 188
Modality, 33–39, 90, 96, 106, 116, 140–141, 145, 174, 178, 182–183
Modal verb, 33–35, 37, 72, 95, 106, 115, 144, 145, 160, 176, 178, 189
Mood, 27, 29, 75–76, 78, 87, 96, 106, 116, 145, 164, 182
Morpheme, 1, 3, 11–17, 103–104, 120, 123, 125, 128, 180–181
Morphology, 2, 7, 28, 104, 120
Multi-word verb, 14, 33–39, 106, 124, 126, 140–141, 143, 145, 182–183

N

Negative, 22, 29, 75, 131, 132, 147, 172, 182
Non-finite, 28, 65–67, 69, 73, 90, 95, 107, 115, 162–164, 176, 178, 183, 188
Non-finite complement clause, 66–67, 69, 162, 176, 181
Noun, 12–17, 19–25, 27, 41, 51, 52, 59, 65–67, 76, 80, 85, 86, 90, 95, 103–105, 115, 123–134, 156, 171, 175, 176, 178–182, 188–190
Noun-complement clause, 59
Noun phrase, 19–25, 27, 35, 41–43, 45, 51, 52, 65–67, 69, 70, 75, 80, 85–88, 90, 95, 104–105, 115, 129–134, 160, 167, 168, 175, 176, 181–182, 188, 189

O

Object, 2, 5, 8, 12, 19, 20, 22, 30, 35, 41–43, 46, 48, 53, 66, 67, 69, 71, 73, 76, 85, 86, 88, 89, 93, 96, 107, 111, 116, 117, 120, 122–124, 129, 130, 133, 147, 150, 159, 160, 162, 164–166, 172, 173, 175, 176, 178, 186, 187, 189, 190
Object complement, 43, 67, 72, 73, 150, 160, 162, 164, 182
Open category, 12, 17, 128

P

Paragraph, 3–5, 11–16, 23, 24, 30–32, 35, 37, 44, 45, 48, 54, 60, 62, 77, 80, 82, 83, 120, 121, 123–127, 133, 135, 136, 139, 140, 150, 153, 156, 168, 170, 174, 178, 187, 188
Parallelism, 78, 81, 111, 168–170, 172, 187, 188
Participle, 28, 66, 71, 72, 176
Part of speech, 12
Passive voice, 76, 78, 90, 168, 171
Past, 23, 29–31, 37, 125, 131, 135, 136, 138–142, 144–146, 149, 156, 167, 168, 171, 172, 175, 177, 178, 182, 189
Past continuous, 144
Past perfect, 135, 136, 139, 144, 168, 182
Past perfect continuous, 29, 182
Perfective aspect, 139
Phrase, xiii, xiv, 1, 14, 19–25, 27, 29, 33, 35, 41–49, 76, 78, 86, 103–105, 107, 113, 120, 121, 128–131, 133–136, 140–142, 146, 148, 150, 161, 168, 169, 176, 187, 190, 193

Postmodification, 20, 21, 23–25, 65, 67, 105, 130–133, 181
Predicate, 51, 52, 67, 76, 85
Predicative, 124
Prefix, 12
Premodification, 20, 23, 24, 129, 132, 181
Preposition, 12, 20, 33, 35, 124, 131
Prepositional phrase, 20, 21, 43, 44, 86, 90, 129, 131, 148, 150, 175, 176
Present, xiv, 4, 7, 29, 31, 32, 52, 72, 99, 125, 131, 135–137, 140–142, 146, 147, 167, 171, 172, 175, 178, 182, 189
Present continuous, 29
Present perfect, 29
Progressive aspect, 28
Pronoun, 12, 20, 21, 42, 68, 71, 86, 87, 90, 95, 105, 115, 128, 130, 161, 163, 170, 171, 175, 178, 181, 189
Proper noun, 14, 86, 123, 189
Punctuation, 75, 77, 80, 90, 169, 176

R

Relative pronoun, 21
Reported clause, 66, 159, 163

S

Semi-modal verb, 29, 34, 95
Sentence, x, xiii, xiv, 1–5, 7, 11–14, 17, 19, 22–24, 27–32, 37, 41, 47, 48, 51, 53, 54, 57–63, 66, 68, 69, 71, 72, 75–83, 85–90, 94–96, 103–105, 107–111, 113–117, 120–122, 126, 128, 130–132, 134, 147, 151–155, 159, 161, 163, 164, 170, 173, 174, 176, 178, 180, 182, 184–190, 193
Simple aspect, 136
Simple past, 139, 172, 182
Simple present, 28, 38
Simple sentence, 57, 60–62, 86, 90, 156–158, 164, 174, 178, 188
Stative verb, 78, 81, 167, 169, 170
Subject, v, xi, xiv, 19, 20, 36, 42, 43, 45, 46, 51–54, 66–69, 71–73, 76, 79, 80, 85, 86, 88, 106, 107, 117, 121, 130, 141, 143, 147, 150–152, 159, 161, 162, 164, 165, 168, 169, 172, 176, 178, 182–185, 190
Subject complement, 43, 66, 151
Subordinate clause, 58, 62, 86, 95, 96, 115, 116, 178, 186

Subordinating conjunction, 58, 157
Subordination, 58, 189
Subordinator, 58, 186
Suffix, 12, 125, 180
Syntactic category, 19, 27, 41, 150
Syntax, 2, 85, 120

T

Tense, 27–32, 66, 87, 90, 95, 105–106, 115, 124, 134–139, 163, 176, 178, 182, 189
Text, v, ix–xiv, 4, 7, 11, 12, 15–17, 31, 32, 34, 35, 37, 45, 48, 56, 62, 75–83, 93–95, 99, 103, 109–111, 113–115, 117, 119, 120, 123, 124, 126, 128, 130, 133, 139, 148, 149, 162, 164, 172, 176, 178, 179, 186–187, 189, 191, 193, 195
Transitive verb, 42, 45, 48, 150, 178, 184, 189
Transitivity, 42–43, 46, 90, 96, 116, 149, 150, 178, 189

V

Verb, 12, 19, 27–39, 41, 52, 59, 66, 75, 86, 95, 105–106, 115, 124
Verb-complement clause, 59, 66
Verb phrase, 24, 27, 41–49, 51, 52, 59, 65, 67, 70, 72, 75, 76, 78, 81, 85–87, 90, 106–107, 140, 145–147, 149, 150, 160, 175, 176, 178, 179, 183–184, 188

W

Word, xii–xiv, 1, 2, 4, 8, 11–17, 19, 23, 28, 30, 32, 34, 37, 41, 43, 45, 58, 60, 76, 77, 80, 81, 85, 93–96, 103–104, 115–117, 120–123, 125–128, 131, 132, 135, 138, 141–143, 145, 150, 153, 157, 159, 161, 164, 166, 167, 169, 172, 174, 180–181, 183, 186–190
Word class, 12

GPSR Compliance
The European Union's (EU) General Product Safety Regulation (GPSR) is a set of rules that requires consumer products to be safe and our obligations to ensure this.

If you have any concerns about our products, you can contact us on

ProductSafety@springernature.com

In case Publisher is established outside the EU, the EU authorized representative is:

Springer Nature Customer Service Center GmbH
Europaplatz 3
69115 Heidelberg, Germany

www.ingramcontent.com/pod-product-compliance
Ingram Content Group UK Ltd.
Pitfield, Milton Keynes, MK11 3LW, UK
UKHW022241230426
12048UKWH00018BA/1400